The Essential Truths

Edited by Den Slattery and Gary Wales

THE ESSENTIAL TRUTHS
Den Slattery and Gary Wales, General Editors

© 1997 by Den Slattery and Gary Wales
Published by Bristol Books, an imprint of Bristol House, Ltd.

First Edition, August 1997

Unless otherwise indicated, all Scripture quotations are from the *Holy Bible, New International Version,* © 1973, 1978, 1984 by the International Bible Society. Used by permission of Zondervan Publishing House.

ISBN: 1-885224-14-1

Printed in the United States of America

Bristol House, Ltd.
P.O. Box 4020
Anderson, Indiana 46013-0020
Phone: 765-644-0856
Fax: 765-622-1045

To order call: 1-800-451-READ (7323)

Dedication

This book has been written during a time when lies, deception, and trickery abound in all of society, including the Church. In this climate, it is hard to know whom to trust, for everyone has an equal opinion and everything seems relative. The only solid truth that people trust is either the result of a scientific study or the findings of a national survey.

However, there is truth apart from science, surveys, and opinions. That TRUTH is found in the Bible and in Jesus Christ. Therefore, this book is dedicated to everyone who is searching for THE TRUTH.

Acknowledgments

We would like to thank the people at Bristol House for believing in this project. Particularly, Sara Anderson and her staff deserve the credit for making this book become a reality. Gary and I have been very thankful for all of the dedicated people who worked with us. Many of the authors are very busy people who are known all over the world, yet they took time out of their schedules because they believed in the importance of this project. May God reward them for their efforts.

We would also like to thank our families for allowing us the extra time away to work on computers or to meet in restaurants hammering out the details. The people in our churches have also been more than patient with us as we have preached each of the "Essential Truths" during our Sunday morning services. And we thank you, the reader, for picking up a copy of this book and reading it.

Finally, we would like to thank the Lord for laying the burden on our hearts to do more than complain about how bad things are in the world and in the Church. With a sense of urgency we felt led to put down on paper what the "Essential Truths" are. Since we began this project people from several other denominations and parachurch groups have also felt led by God to do the same thing. In looking at the books, magazine articles and tracts that we have discovered, it is amazing how similar our conclusions are in spite of different backgrounds. I believe that God has been leading all of us to write about TRUTH because there is so much deception and heresy being taught.

It is our prayer that you would embrace the truth.

Den Slattery and Gary Wales

Contents

Foreword

Ideas have consequences. What we believe, deeply believe, determines how we live.

In an article in the June 16, 1997 issue of *Christianity Today,* Dr. Jerry Walls makes the case that the diminished belief in heaven and hell is accountable for the moral relativism of our day, the fading of virtue. The diminished belief in heaven and hell is due to vague and fuzzy notions about God. Heaven and hell bring God into the picture. "And at once everything looks different. No compromise is necessary. If we are eternal persons whose lives have an eternal context, then self-interest dictates that we follow the laws of heaven. Heaven is the true fulfillment of all human desire. And so without seeing ourselves as heaven's citizens, we cannot order our desires the right way. We will desire lesser goods (the goodness of sexual acts) over higher ones (the goodness of fidelity). In other words, we cannot redefine our wants without challenging the secular definition of who we are. So the moral significance of hell is not to serve as a threat to deter uncivil behavior. Hell in its adjudication is the judgment of God, but in its nature it is the intrinsic consequence of pursuing the wrong means to happiness. It is the natural outcome of not considering carefully who we are and profoundly pursuing what will truly satisfy us" (p. 24).

Ideas have consequences. What we believe, deeply believe, determines how we live. This has special meaning for the Church. For instance, what we think about Jesus Christ will determine what we do about evangelism. If we don't have confidence in the Gospel, if we are not solidly convicted about the uniqueness of Christ, it is not likely that evangelism will have much priority in our personal ministry and/or in our church.

Take it one step further: What we do about evangelism is shaped by what we think about grace. If we believe in the rich tradition of Wesleyan thought that grace is universally offered, but not universally received, how we witness will be affected. Our proclamation of the Gospel will take on an urgency because we are dealing with eternal implications. There is eternal judgment to consider.

One other word about ideas and consequences in the Christian life and the Church. We come full circle: what we think Jesus Christ can do for persons will determine what we do about evangelism.

The contributors to this volume believe with me that ideas have consequences. So they have written a collection of essays on *Essential Truths*. And the "essentials" are addressed—the heart of the Christian faith. If the book does nothing more than call congregations across the Methodist connection to consider these essentials, it will have served a great purpose.

Most denominations, including my own, the United Methodist Church, are in crisis. It is a crisis of faith and a crisis of identity. We have lost a common voice that says with confidence, "This we believe," and we have lost a common mission which acts with zeal: this is who we are and this we will do.

It is my prayer that this volume will move us along in recovering our faith and identity.

Maxie D. Dunnam
President, Asbury Theological Seminary

Introduction

It matters what we believe! Our beliefs will determine how we live, what we live for, and even what we are willing to die for. How we invest our time, talents and money are all affected by what we believe. Our self-esteem, purpose in life, and the goals we set for ourselves are often determined by what we believe. And most importantly, our beliefs will determine our eternal destiny. Therefore, it is imperative to come to a knowledge of the truth.

Pilate, who served as a type of governor, once asked Jesus the question, "What is truth?" Had Pilate been following Jesus's ministry he would have heard Jesus describe "Truth" as the "Word of God" (John 17:17). Jesus was the embodiment of that "Word" (John 1:1–12). Therefore, if God says something is true, who are we to correct him? God's Word (the Bible) is the standard by which all else is judged.

This is a book dealing with the great doctrines of the Bible. Many people today say that it doesn't matter what we believe, as long as we are sincere. That couldn't be further from the truth. What we believe affects every other area of life. For example, people may say they believe that they can fly after watching too many Superman movies. But when they jump off a ten-story building, their sincere beliefs will be overcome by the "truth" of gravity. In the same way, there are truths established by God that will never change. This book you now hold in your hands is an attempt to reveal a few of God's "essential truths" recorded and preserved for all time in the Bible.

Each article is written by a different author. All of the authors are leaders in the Church and are people of integrity and faith. It is important that you know that none of those authors, including Den Slattery and Gary Wales (the general editors), are making any money on this book. They have all donated their time and talents out of their love for the Church and because they see that there is a great need for people to rediscover the "essential truths" of God's Book.

The general editors of this text, Den Slattery and Gary Wales, worked with a variety of Christian leaders to explore the essential truths of our faith.

Chapter 1

Why We Believe

by Den Slattery

People today don't seem to know what to believe. Our society is so corrupt that it has affected every profession from teachers to judges, from generals to doctors, from the police to the news anchors, and from garbage collectors all the way to the president of the United States. No profession, as a whole, appears to be trustworthy. It hasn't always been that way in America. Earlier in this century people trusted doctors, teachers, pastors, and even movie stars. But the world we live in today is very different. It seems that almost everyone lies, cheats, steals, and surrenders to immorality. No one seems trustworthy. Is it any wonder that we don't demand high standards of morality, honesty, and integrity in our leaders?

In a society where crime is at an all-time high and integrity is at an all-time low, Americans have come to believe that there is no absolute truth. Yet we cry out for answers—"Why are people so cruel?" "Why are there wars?" "Why isn't education solving our problems of poverty, welfare, crime, injustice, gangs, teen pregnancy, AIDS, prejudice, and rape?" "Why do our lives seem to lack purpose?" "Why are our families falling apart?" "Why is there so much divorce?"

For a generation that has rejected God, it's amazing how many people in our world are searching for exactly what God offers. He offers peace, purpose, hope, love, life, deliverance, salvation, and truth. Yet what is even more amazing is that many people who faithfully attend church in America don't understand even the basics of the faith. While the world is crying out for answers, the church wavers in unbelief. The present American culture seems to parallel Nazi Germany in many ways. One of those ways is in the church's rejection of orthodox truth. This book is written to help restate the core of orthodox Christian belief.

Why Christians Believe

People today are often critical of Christianity and the Bible. They ask—"Why should we believe you?" "What makes your opinion any better than ours?" Those are valid questions. But perhaps we should first ask, "*Why* do we believe?"

As Christians, we have made a *decision* to believe that Jesus Christ is the Son of the living God, who died on a cross for our sins and rose from the dead so that we could have the free gift of eternal life. It was a choice we made based on the truth we discovered. That truth is rooted in the Bible, history, and our personal experience. Therefore, it seems reasonable to those of us who have embraced it, but strange to others who have rejected it (1 Corinthians 1:18–31).

The Bible

What we believe about God, Jesus, heaven, hell, and whatever else, has been affected, first and foremost, by our view of Scripture. For example, if we say the Bible is filled with errors and myths, then it stands to reason that we will be skeptical and even critical about almost anything it says. On the other hand, if we embrace the Bible as the true Word of God, we will treasure every word of it. Billy Graham once admitted that he struggled with this very issue. Some scholars had told him he couldn't trust the Bible. Billy went to God with his questions and doubts and felt God led him to reject the doubts and trust the Bible. He later said, "I haven't had any problem with that issue since that day." Many of our pulpits in America are filled with pastors who have been taught by liberal scholars that the Bible is not to be trusted. Is it any wonder, therefore, that there is confusion among churchgoing people about what to believe?

People

Our beliefs are not only affected by our view of the Bible, they are also drastically influenced by other people. People from our past have played a part in making us who we are today. They could be our family members, friends, heroes, teachers, the media, or even people in the past who have jotted down their ideas for us to read. Everyone is influenced by someone. Therefore, no one is totally objective. In seminary, our professors talked frequently about the need for us to be totally objective when we approach the Scriptures, problems in life, and people. But over the years I have learned that no one is totally objective about anything. We have all been influenced by others. The influence of other people has affected us and actually helps us to decipher our world. Some refer to this as our worldview.

Personal Experience

Yet even beyond the influence of others is our own personal experience. The events in our lives play an important role in forming our belief systems. To trust in our own experience is often a powerful force. However, it is possible for our beliefs to change if they seem to be unacceptable among our peers.

Reason

In the final analysis, we want to know that what we believe is reasonable. Does it ring true when others hear it? Is it worth believing? Does it make sense, given the evidence? We want to

think that our decisions about what to believe are based on sound
critical thinking.

The Bottom Line

Therefore, we contend that our beliefs are determined by
our view of the Bible, our personal experiences, the influence of others in our past (history), and whether or not it
seems reasonable, given the evidence available to us at the
time.

John Wesley, the founder of Methodism, determined Christian truth on the basis of four factors: Scripture, tradition, reason, and experience (this is known as the "Wesleyan Quadrilateral"). Wesley held that the Bible was always to be the foundation and final standard of all of our beliefs. However, many of
today's church leaders often exalt reason and experience above
the Bible. This practice frequently results in embracing doctrines
that are in direct contradiction to what the Bible teaches. History
records that when the Bible is rejected as the standard for truth,
heresy is not far behind.

In this book on "Essential Truths," we will be dealing with
the following subjects:

Truth	The Bible	God
Jesus	Holy Spirit	Satan
Eternity	Holiness	Church
Mission	Church Growth	Prayer
Disciplemaking	People	Salvation

We will also include a statement on how to know God. These
subjects have been chosen because they have been upheld by
almost all groups of Christians as central to the faith. Some might
argue that church growth is a modern phenomenon, but the book
of Acts is the main source book for that subject, since it is filled
with stories of the growth of the early church.

All of the authors in this book are actively engaged in some kind of ministry to help the church. Our prayer is that Jesus Christ will be exalted and that the church will grow in the knowledge of the truth.

Questions

1. What are our beliefs based upon?
2. Is there any hard evidence to prove that we believe the truth?
3. What was John Wesley's Quadrilateral? Is the Wesleyan Quadrilateral still helpful today?
4. Have you ever believed something that wasn't true? Were you sincere?
5. What part does reason play in Christianity?
6. What makes our beliefs right?
7. Is there truth in other religions? What makes Christianity different?

Den Slattery   A Pastor and Army Chaplain, Rev. Slattery served in a special Marine C.A.P. Unit in Vietnam from 1969–1970 and in the Army, (Avionics) from 1971–1975 with tours in both Vietnam and Korea. He received his M.Div. from Anderson University, with emphasis on Pastoral Ministry, and is just completing his D.Min., with emphasis on Church Growth, from Trinity Evangelical Divinity School. In 1996 he was awarded the Denman Evangelism Award by the West Michigan Conference in conjunction with the Foundation of Evangelism. He and Karen, his wife of 17 years, live in Marcellus, Michigan, where they are homeschooling their four children. He is the author of From the Point to the Cross *and several articles and tracts.*

Chapter 2

The Importance of Truth

by James V. Heidinger II

For years we have heard the claim that the Christian church must have "a preferential option for the poor." And whenever the church has been faithful to the gospel, it has most certainly shown a profound and practical concern for the poor.

However, a concern for the poor can be thwarted by a misunderstood and misguided benevolence about what will actually help the poor. Sometimes our well-meaning efforts at charity can actually do more harm than good. What the church must have, in this and all of its concerns, is a preferential option for the truth.

But in recent years something has happened to the church's interest in and understanding of truth, and it's important that we are aware of it. Increasingly, in our discussions about matters of faith, we hear about personal experiences and feelings, but very little about truth. We hear much about consensus building, but little about obeying the truth. In our passion for dialogue, it seems that the benefit is mainly in the experience of dialogue itself, with little anticipation of or interest in the discovery of truth.

The Apostle Paul urged Timothy to be a workman "who correctly handles the word of truth" (2 Timothy 2.15). He reminded
Timothy about two teachers, Hymenaeus and Philetus, "who have
wandered away from the truth" and as a result "they destroy the
faith of some" (2:18). Mishandling the truth can be destructive
to the faith of the church. The church's stewardship of truth is a
serious matter, indeed.

I was reminded of the importance of truth in the life of the
church while attending the solemn service of consecration for
four new United Methodist Bishops at the conclusion of the
North Central Jurisdictional Conference recently. During the
liturgy of consecration, the four newly elected bishops were
reminded, "As servants of the whole Church, you are called to
preach and teach the truth of the gospel to all God's people."
They were then asked several questions, including, "Will you
guard the faith, order, liturgy, doctrine, and discipline of the
Church against all that is contrary to God's Word?" Clearly,
bishops (and all pastors for that matter) must "guard" and "correctly handle the word of truth."

This helps us understand why the Christian church has placed
such great importance on the study of doctrine, at least, it did up
until the last half of the twentieth century. Alister E. McGrath,
professor of theology at Oxford, reminds us of the role doctrine
should play in the life of the church: "Christian doctrine aims to
describe the way things are. It is concerned to tell the truth, in
order that we may enter into and act upon that truth. . . . It [doc-
trine] draws a firm line of demarcation between a false church,
which answers to the pressures of the age, and a true church,
which is obedient and responsible to God, as he has revealed
himself in Jesus Christ."[1]

The danger of losing hold of the truth is that the church will
begin taking its cues from the society around it. McGrath warns

---

[1] Alister E. McGrath, *Understanding Doctrine,* Grand Rapids: Zondervan Publishing
House, p. 12.

of the pathetic results when this happens: "A church which despises or neglects doctrine (truth) comes perilously close to losing its reason for existence, and may simply lapse into a comfortable conformity with the world—or whatever part of the world it happens to feel most at home with. Its agenda is set by the world; its presuppositions are influenced by the world; its outlook mirrors that of the world. There are few more pathetic sights than a church wandering aimlessly from one 'meaningful' issue to another in a desperate search for relevance in the eyes of the world."[2] What a vivid description of a church that wanders away from the truth.

Christian doctrine makes truth claims. It speaks with clear affirmations about reality, the order of things, about the way things really are. Things that are true are, therefore, reliable, constant, certain, and in accordance with facts. It is what we know as "objective truth."

More recently, existentialism has stressed the subjective character of truth. That is, truth is something very personal or individual, something I must experience for myself. The focus is placed more on experiences than on objective truth.

I remember when I first discovered this new approach to truth. A group of United Methodist evangelicals published a White Paper addressing social and theological issues that we felt needed to be addressed by our annual conference. The paper was circulated widely and aroused considerable controversy. As a result, our annual conference authorized a representative task force of 24 persons to meet four times during the next year to discuss the paper's contents. We were encouraged. At the first meeting of the task force, after introductions had been made, several members charged that the White Paper made claims about United Methodism that were not documented adequately. So the task force agreed that at the next meeting, representatives from the evangelical authors of the document would bring documentation

---

[2] Ibid., p. 13–14.

of their charges that would provide a basis for discussion. However, when the dialogue group gathered for the second meeting to review the documentation of the evangelicals, the chairman announced that rather than pursue the specific contents of the paper, the task force would instead spend its time sharing faith journeys. The task force never got around to a careful discussion of the specific charges of the White Paper. Sharing faith journeys, it appeared, had become more valued than wrestling with important theological issues.

This subjective or existential view of truth gets credited, and rightly so, with the methodology of theological liberalism. Liberal theology is usually dated from Friedrich Schleiermacher (d. 1834) and later as revised by Ludwig Feuerbach (d. 1872). The latter argued that all religious claims are "projections" of human experience, longings, and fantasies. Thus, says Richard John Neuhaus, "The essential conflict between orthodox Christianity and this brand of liberalism is over the question of *truth*."[3] Neuhaus goes on to say that most liberals "operate with the subjectivist assumption that truth means *what is true for you.* They are utilitarians in their belief that truth is *what works.* The end toward which such truth is supposed to 'work' is the maximizing of the expression of the *autonomous self.* Truth, in this view, is a human construct. Truth is, quite precisely, a fabrication in the sense that it is manufactured by us."[4]

This subjectivism of truth has become widely accepted in the mainline churches in America under such terms as "theological pluralism" and "diversity." It has left many denominations approaching Christian doctrine with a cafeteria-line approach. One can go through the line and select those portions of Christian doctrine that one believes to be "true for me" and pass by those doctrines that one dislikes. Someone has defined "theological

---

[3] Richard John Neuhaus, quoted in "What Do Liberals Believe Today?", *Good News* (March/April 1991): 15.

[4] *Ibid.*

pluralism" facetiously, saying, "Pluralism is the belief that all opinions have validity except those that claim to be true." There is more truth in that statement than most liberals would admit.

This kind of liberalism is insidious, in that it excludes the whole idea of normative truth, which is so foundational to classic Christianity. It is also insidious in that it will always appear to be winsome and tolerant while orthodoxy will appear "narrow," "mean-spirited," and "uncompromising." This is not difficult to understand. For the liberal theologian, compromise, tolerance, and inclusiveness are the norm. The liberal would say, "Why don't we quit fussing over doctrine and just agree with one another in love?" One radical Episcopal Church bishop has even referred to doctrine as "the ties that bind and blind." Others will say, "With such critical social problems facing our communities, we can't afford the luxury of bickering about doctrinal questions. Let's get on with ministering to people's needs."

This kind of compromise sounds so appealing, so sensible. If doctrine simply "binds and blinds," why spend much time with it? The problem is that orthodox Christians believe doctrinal truth to be of foundational importance. If the foundation is not right, the entire structure will not stand. Orthodox believers aren't about to compromise doctrinal truth with appeals to tolerance and broadmindedness, no matter how popular such an approach may be.

In many of the mainline churches today, our leaders have embraced the relativism of our culture and of theological liberalism so thoroughly that the very concept of absolute truth has been abandoned. Truth, it is said, is a construct of one's group, tribe, or tradition. But it is never considered truth for all. To affirm normative truth is viewed as exclusive, in that it denies contrary truth claims that others may hold. Thus, we marginalize or exclude them by our claims. As a result, there is no universal point of reference for our self-understanding and moral decisions. We are like mariners adrift with no charts or compass, lost in a sea of relativism, with everyone on board uttering opinions about which way the ship should sail.

This kind of liberalism will find it difficult to contend for any truth whatsoever. Maciej Zieba reminds us, "Liberalism that excludes truth is unable to contend for its own truth, and is thus left defenseless in the face of totalitarianisms that claim to be *the* truth. Liberal societies that exclude or stifle communities that bear witness to truth unwittingly end up by acting as though they possess the absolute truth—the existence of which they theoretically deny."[5] The obvious danger here, of course, is when a group like the Third Reich in Germany during World War II makes absolutist truth claims that must be refuted, not with mere opinions, but with normative, widely held, and understood truth claims. At such a time, subjective or personalized views will be of little value.

As Christians, we are called to follow the One who said, "I am the truth" (John 14:6). We are not only to tell the truth, but to live it as well. This will often mean doing so against a contemporary cultural tide which opposes us. Knowing the truth will help Christians as well as the church avoid falling into serious error.

Several years ago I read an account of a challenge given by Catholic Cardinal Ratzinger to a group of American archbishops. In his address he lamented the fact that many of his church's theologians and academicians had adopted the relativism of the present day. And sadly, he noted, the bishops are failing to challenge it. They are not bringing the theologians and academicians to a point of decision, confronting them with "the authority of the truth." Then Cardinal Ratzinger said something that moved me deeply: "It is the hallmark of truth to be worth suffering for. The faithful have a right to know which theologians are right and which are wrong. This kind of authoritative teaching," he insisted, "is the job of bishops— even at the cost of popularity, *even at the cost of martyrdom*" (emphasis mine). This was a powerful reminder to me that

---

[5] Maciej Zieba, "The Liberalism that We Need," *First Things,* no. 40 (February 1994): 27.

many believers across the years have given their very lives for being faithful to the truth.

Paul urged not only Timothy, but all of us who follow the Lord Jesus, to be workers "who correctly handle the word of truth." Let's be sure we have a preferential option for the truth. If we do, we may become workers "who do not need to be ashamed."

Questions

1. What is truth? Does truth matter? Explain.
2. How do we discover truth?
3. Are there any absolute truths?
4. Why did Jesus say, "I am the truth . . ."?
5. How does the Bible fit into our discussion about truth?
6. Have you always been truthful?
7. Does it matter if our leaders are truthful? Explain.

James V. Heidinger II President and Publisher of Good News *magazine since 1981, Rev. Heidinger leads the influential Good News movement as it works toward spiritual renewal in the United Methodist Church. He is the author of* United Methodist Renewal: What Will It Take? *and editor of* Basic United Methodist Beliefs. *He received his Th.M. in 1967 from Asbury Theological Seminary and his D.Min. in 1973 from Wesley Theological Seminary with emphasis in the area of the History of Christian Social Thought. He and his wife of 26 years, Joanne, live with their three children in Nicholasville, Kentucky.*

Chapter 3

The Authority of the Bible

by Gary Wales

In the early 1990s, I was part of a weekly Bible study group with four or five United Methodist pastors. Our group discovered that a young pastor in a nearby parish was seeking to be ordained. She had completed seminary and was writing her final theology paper which she had to present to the Board of Ordained Ministry for approval. So we invited her to come to our Bible study to share her theology paper with the group. That way we could offer our insights and suggestions as she prepared to stand before the board. We had the best of intentions and simply wanted to be supportive.

After reading the young woman's paper, I was truly confused. Though it was perhaps 30 pages long, I saw scant mention of Jesus Christ. In the presence of the entire Bible study group I asked, "Where does Jesus fit into your theology?" She said, "He doesn't." I asked, "How then is a person saved?" She said, "Anyone who believes in God is saved." I said, "Does that include Muslims, Hindus, and even idol worshipers who believe in some kind of a god?" She responded, "Yes. It looks like you have found me out." I was horrified. She had openly denied the most foundational truth of the Bible, that Jesus Christ is the only Savior But about two months later she was ordained to the ministry on the basis of that very same theology paper. Why? I guess because she was very articulate in defense of beliefs that should have been indefensible in a Christian church.

As I have told that story, lay people are especially troubled. They assume that the Bible constitutes the standard for theology and behavior among pastors. They assume that when a young man or woman goes off to seminary, he or she will be taught to build a theology and worldview on the foundation of the Scriptures. Yet in large numbers, seminary students and pastors have turned from the truth to follow "gods of their own imagination." If they don't like what the Bible says about Jesus, or hell, or sin, or any other doctrine, they simply reject it. How can they do such a thing? Quite simply, they deny the accuracy and authority of God's Word, the Bible. I'll always remember the time when I was speaking with another pastor about Jesus Christ. This pastor denied the deity of Jesus. When I turned to Scripture to show him why I believed in the doctrine, he said, "Don't bother. I don't care what the Bible says. I don't believe it."

Sometimes people in the parish come to me and ask how things could have gone so far from truth in the church today. How can the plain truths of Scripture be so easily discarded by those who are commissioned to preach? My answer is that it actually happened very slowly. It began years ago when the authority of Scripture was challenged in a few areas. But compromise of the truth spreads like cancer. It knows no boundaries. People come to believe that if the Bible is unreliable on a few points, then it must be unreliable through and through. They incorrectly assume that the Bible erred about Jonah being swallowed by a great fish. Then, they incorrectly assume that the Bible also erred about who Jesus Christ really is. It's like that old saying, "If you let the camel stick his nose in the tent, soon you will be sharing your tent with a camel."

Does It Matter What You Believe?

Some people would have us believe that there are no "absolutes" when it comes to truth as long as you are sincere in your beliefs. They say, "You may believe the Bible, or the Muslim Koran, or personal opinions, or whatever works for you. But I believe what works for me." Such a statement is not well thought out. If, for example, one person concurs with Scripture in believing that Jesus Christ is the *only* Savior, and another person believes that Jesus Christ is merely one of many saviors, both cannot be right. The two positions are mutually exclusive. For one to be right, the other must be wrong. The major doctrines of Scripture are not relative. They are absolute statements that must be either right or wrong. And it matters what we believe because the Bible claims that our eternal destiny depends upon it.

Jeffrey Dahmer was a mentally troubled man who seduced young men, killed them, mutilated their corpses, ate their flesh, and even practiced necrophilia. After being found guilty of these heinous crimes, he was interviewed from prison in January 1994 by Stone Phillips of NBC news. Stone asked Jeffrey Dahmer how he could do such deeds. Dahmer said that when you don't believe in God, there are no rules. Jeffrey Dahmer was mentally ill, but actually he made a good point. Who makes the rules? Do the rules change from person to person? And if truth is relative, then what is wrong today may be right tomorrow. Indeed, that which is wrong today may actually one day become a religious duty, if truth is relative and evolves over time. But God's truth does not evolve. Jesus said, "Heaven and earth will pass away, but my words will never pass away." The Bible is a book of absolutes.

An Infallible Book

The Bible claims to be an infallible book, meaning that it is incapable of error. Within its pages we find statements like the following, "Every word of God is flawless . . ." (Proverbs 30:5). That means that the Bible is totally trustworthy in all that it intends to teach. But we must realize that infallibility is not the same as "literalism." Just like all good literature, the Bible uses metaphor and other figures of speech that teach great truths, but were never meant to be taken literally. For example, the Bible says, "The Lord is my rock" (Psalm 18:2). He is not literally a rock in the yard, but he is powerful and strong like a rock. Jesus said: "I am the gate" (John 10:9). He is not literally a gate on hinges, but he is the only way to heaven. Such teaching is truthful but not literal. Figures of speech do not diminish the Bible's authority.

We also use figures of speech in our modern language. I may say to my friends, "I'm going to hit the road at 8 P.M." That does not mean that I am going to pound my fist on the pavement. Virtually everyone would understand that I was planning to depart at 8 P.M. If I did indeed depart then, my words would have been truthful. When the meteorologist declares that the sun will rise at 7:01 A.M., he is not speaking a falsehood, though the sun does not literally rise; our earth rotates. In a similar way, not all parts of the Bible are intended to be taken literally. But all parts of the Bible are completely truthful and without error in all that is intended to be taught.

How do we know that the Bible is true? There are a number of solid reasons to subscribe to the view of infallibility:

1. **God is the author.** The Bible is not a human invention but comes from God. God did give it through human channels, but Scripture declares that he was the Author behind the authors. The Bible says, "All Scripture is God-breathed" (2 Timothy 3:16). Further, the Bible says, "God is not a man, that he should lie, nor a son of man, that he should change his mind" (Numbers 23:19).

2. **Fulfilled prophecy proves the Bible.** The birth, life, and death of Jesus Christ were prophesied hundreds of years before they were fulfilled. A good deal of prophecy concerning the return of Jesus and the end of the age has yet to be fulfilled.

3. **The Bible is internally consistent.** The Bible was written over a period of about 1600 years, by about 40 different authors (from kings to fishermen), in three different languages (Hebrew, Aramaic, Greek), on three different continents (Asia, Africa, Europe). Yet the Bible speaks with great consistency from Genesis to Revelation concerning the great doctrines of our faith.

4. **The Bible changes lives.** God speaks to us through his Word. He uses that Word to accomplish his purposes: "[God's Word] will not return to me empty, but will accomplish what I desire and achieve the purpose for which I sent it" (Isaiah 55:11). God's Word can transform the most hardened sinner into a compliant and repentant follower of Christ.

It is true that many pastors today do not believe in the infallibility of Scripture. But those preachers who do not trust the Bible are in effect saying, "Don't trust the Scriptures, but trust my opinions as I preach to you." In the final analysis one trusts God's Word or the opinions of people. We either follow the God of the Bible or the god of our imaginations. In my first parish there was a new Christian named Ron. One day Ron said to me, "Pastor, if I can't believe all of the Bible, I can't believe any of it." I thought to myself, "Here is a wise man. He has not been a Christian for long, but he is off to a real good start."

The Greatest Crisis of Our Day

Imagine that you are an employee in a major corporation and you love your company. But suppose that your company experiences a financial loss for 30 consecutive years. Suppose that after 30 years your share of the market is reduced fully by a third, but some of your competitors are growing steadily, year after year. You naturally conclude that you are in the midst of a corporate catastrophe and that you are doing something very wrong.

This analogy may be applied to the Christian denomination that I love and of which I am a part: The United Methodist Church.

In 1968, The United Methodist Church had approximately 12.5 million members. Twenty eight years later, in 1996, we have only about 8.5 million members. While our denomination has been losing members, many other denominations, such as the Southern Baptists, have grown. Why? We United Methodists are nice people. We are inclusive of all races and classes of people, as we should be. We have been innovative in trying program after program. But we have failed in the most basic principle of all. We have failed to believe and preach the full counsel of God's Word. God uses the Bible to change hearts and cause growth. Anything less than a high view of Scripture, the preaching of salvation through faith in Christ, and a radical obedience to all of God's Word will keep us on our present path of decline. God says in his Word: "Those who honor me I will honor, but those who despise me will be disdained" (1 Samuel 2:30).

How important is the Bible? Is it relevant for today? Absolutely! Not only is it relevant, but the future well-being of the church and our nation rests on our collective knowledge of and compliance to God's Word. Is that an extreme statement? Perhaps. Yet consider the promises and warnings that God attached to his Word among Old Testament Israelites: "If you fully obey the Lord your God and carefully follow all his commands . . . all these blessings will come upon you. . . . However, if you do not obey the Lord your God and do not carefully follow all his commands . . . all these curses will come upon you and overtake you. . . ." (See Deuteronomy 28:1–2 and the entire chapter.)

The Formula for Successful Living

Moses had been used by God to deliver the Israelites from bondage, and then to lead them through the wilderness to the Promised Land. But before entering that land, Moses died. His successor was Joshua. It was his job to lead the people into the Promised Land. There were to be battles and trials, but God graciously gave Joshua the formula for success. God said, "Do not let this Book of the Law depart from your mouth; meditate on it day and night, so that you may be careful to do everything written in it. Then you will be prosperous and successful (Joshua 1:8). This formula required Joshua to do four things:

1. **Joshua had to *know* God's Word.** "Do not let this Book . . . depart." In other words, Joshua had to hold it, read it, study it, and let its precepts become his worldview. The Bible is not to be some revered relic that lies on a shelf. We must use it. Unfortunately, we live in an age of great biblical ignorance. Even many pastors do not know the basics of God's Word. Many pastors couldn't quote ten verses of Scripture or even name the Ten Commandments in order if their lives depended on it. Why? They see little value in knowing a book that they do not believe in.

2. **Joshua had to *talk* about God's Word.** ". . . from your mouth." Many of God's people feel comfortable in conversing about almost any subject, whether business, sports, or leisure; but they are afraid to talk about God's Word. Often it is fear of ridicule or rejection that silences God's people. But Jesus sternly warns his people, "If anyone is ashamed of me . . . the Son of Man will be ashamed of him. . ." (Mark 8:38). We must not keep the Word of life to ourselves; we must share it.

3. **Joshua had to *meditate* on God's Word.** ". . . meditate on it day and night." Biblical meditation is not the least bit like transcendental meditation (TM) of New Age and Eastern religions. In TM people seek to empty their minds and become "one" with the cosmos. That is not at all what God desires for his people. Nowhere does God condone the emptying of our minds. Biblical meditation is the opposite of TM. Biblical meditation is the "filling" of our minds with the Word of God. This kind of meditation is focusing on Scripture, dwelling on it, mulling it over in our minds, and asking the Holy Spirit to help us apply it to our lives. To put it simply, God's approved meditation is to concentrate deeply on his Word.

Unfortunately, the art of meditation is not generally under-stood or practiced in our day.

4. **Joshua had to *obey* God's Word.** "do everything written in it." At the time of this writing, my wife and I have five chil-dren. We love our children dearly. But our household is not a democracy where the children can conspire to outvote the parents. Even if we had 20 children, my one vote would out-weigh their 20 votes. For the family to succeed, the parents must be in charge. We set the rules; we administer the disci-pline; we determine the daily dinner menu. In a similar way, the kingdom of God is not a democracy where we can vote God's rules in or out. It is a kingdom that is ruled by a King (that's why it's not called the "democracy of God"). The bot-tom line is that God has spoken, and he requires obedience to his Word. Disobedience always leads to failure and punish-ment in the long run. Obedience always leads to successful Christian living and spiritual blessing.

Conclusion

In presenting "The Essential Truths," the Bible must come first. Why? If you begin to construct your theological convic-tions on the authority and infallibility of Scripture, you will be building upon a solid foundation. You may still have questions. You may still hold wrong views. But as you acquire a greater understanding of God's Word, your doctrines will begin to con-form to the Truth that God wants each of us to embrace. But if you believe that your own opinions, or the writings of fallible people, are to be trusted more than God, you will be building on a crumbling foundation. Opinions are fickle. Scholars, each with his or her own bias, are also fickle. The wisdom of today be-comes the foolishness of tomorrow. But God's Word, ancient that it is, remains eternally true and relevant. As God declares in his Word: ". . . all men are like grass, and all their glory is like the flowers of the field; the grass withers and the flowers fall, but the word of the Lord stands forever" (1 Peter 1:24–25).

Questions

1. How do we know the Bible is true? Why do you trust it?
2. Why is it important to study the Bible?
3. What was the formula for success given in Joshua 1:8-9?
4. What is your favorite book of the Bible? Why? Do you have a favorite verse? What is it?
5. Do you remember the first Bible you owned? Do you still have it?
6. What caused you to start studying the Bible? Do you still read it? Do you follow a plan?
7. Are your beliefs rooted in the Bible? Give an example.

Gary S. Wales   *Pastor of Trowbridge United Methodist Church since 1994, Rev. Wales received his M.Div. from Gordon-Conwell Theological Seminary. He and Cindy, his wife of 14 years, live with their five children in Otsego, Michigan. He received a degree from General Motors Institute and worked for the automaker for several years before entering the ministry.*

Chapter 4

God

by Craig L. Adams

When I was in college, it was fashionable to be skeptical of the existence of God. Many of my friends claimed to be agnostic. They said they had no idea whether God existed or not, but they lived as if God did not exist. Many people live that way. They ask, "Where is God?" Since they can't see him with the naked eye, they assume he doesn't exist.

I can assure you, God is not hard to find. The evidence of God's presence and power is all around us. Furthermore, the Bible tells us that God wants to be known, and most importantly, that there is a way to know him.

Belief in God is not difficult. He has left his fingerprints in the complex world he has created. The evidence is all around us. It's in the oceans filled with life in all forms; it's in the stars and planets we observe on a clear night; it's evident in the great variety of animals, birds, reptiles, and insects; and it's evident in human beings. We can see God's handiwork by the order and complexity in our world. Throughout history, people have held to a belief in God. They haven't always understood everything about God, but people on every continent know intuitively that there is someone greater in the universe.

We are not alone in this world. There is a God who created us and is concerned about us. The Bible indicates that he has a plan and purpose for our lives. Therefore, we are not an accident of evolution. Many modern scientists freely admit that they can't explain life on earth without acknowledging the existence of a greater creative Intelligence behind it all. A strong case can be made for the logic of a belief in God as the Creator of the world. But, for Christians, belief in God is more than this.

God is revealed to us in the Bible. To those of us who believe in God, he is far more than just an idea. God is a reality in our lives. We don't just speak of God in the language of philosophy and abstract theology. We have an ongoing relationship with God.

When I was a teenager I heard an evangelist tell me that God could be a reality in my life. He said we were all incomplete until we found a relationship with God through Jesus Christ. He said we needed forgiveness. We needed to be "born again" into the family of God. He said God wanted to forgive us and walk with us through life. I knew I needed something; if there was a God, I needed him. Nervous and afraid, I went to the altar rail to pray. I had no real faith in that moment. I prayed, "God, if you are really there, I need you." But, God met me where I was, and God has been a reality in my life ever since.

I have discovered that we can know God personally through Jesus Christ. People who have repented of their sins and found forgiveness in Jesus are called Christians. To the Christian, God is not simply an idea or a distant and impersonal being. Nor is he just a philosophical concept. God is real and the Bible tells us that he wants to have a relationship with us.

Faith in Christ puts anyone in touch with God. Jesus came to forge a relationship of forgiveness, grace, and love between people and God. He came to reveal God's love and his desire to restore our broken relationship. In sending Jesus into the world God provided a way for us to have a relationship with the One who created us.

It is a wonderful and amazing thing that the God who created us—and created a universe beyond our comprehension—wants to have a relationship with us.

What Do We Know About God?

I. One God

There is only one God. Behind the existence of everything lies one Creator—who created it all through a greatness and power we cannot begin to comprehend. In John 17:3 Jesus calls him "the only true God." In Deuteronomy 6:4 we read: "Hear, O Israel: The Lord our God, the Lord is one."

We can never completely understand everything about God because God is an infinite and all-powerful being. God is greater than anything our minds can conceive. We can never fully describe God. We can know many things about God's nature and character, but we cannot fully comprehend all that God is.

God is the Creator. Everything owes its existence to God. God's power is awesome (Deuteronomy 7:21). Everything that exists in this universe was created through the will of God (Revelation 4:11).

God is not a man. God is not like any created being. There is no other being that can compare to God. Sometimes the Bible speaks of God as being like a king (Psalms 24:10), or like a father (Isaiah 64:8), or like a rock (Deuteronomy 32 :4), or like a mother eagle (Deuteronomy. 32:11). But, none of these images expresses everything that is true of God. The nations that surrounded Israel had religions that spoke of gods and goddesses. Their deities were sexual beings. But the God of Israel made it clear that he was not to be understood in this way. God does not have a physical form or body as we do (Deuteronomy. 4:15). God is like no other being in the universe: "How great you are, O sovereign Lord! There is no one like you, and there is no God but you, as we have heard with our own ears" (2 Samuel 7:22). "Great is the Lord, and most worthy of praise; his greatness no one can fathom" (Psalms 145:3).

The only reason we know anything about God is because God has revealed it. God wants us to know him. We understand God through the Bible. First, God revealed his will, character, and purpose to Israel. Then God revealed himself to the world in Jesus Christ. The Bible is the written record of what God has revealed.

II. Three in One

The New Testament speaks of God as: Father, Son, and Holy Spirit. Thus, the one God has chosen to reveal himself as three persons. While this is a difficult concept, it is an important one. There is community and interaction within the very character of God. In some way that we cannot fully understand, God has a type of companionship within himself!

The doctrine of the Trinity is practical. It is not simply a doctrine; it is an invitation into the communion that is the very nature of God. We are invited into a life of oneness with both God and with other people who are believers. This oneness reflects the nature of God. So, in John 17:21 Jesus prayed for his disciples "that all of them may be one, Father, just as you are in me and I am in you. May they also be in us so that the world may believe that you have sent me." The doctrine of the Trinity is an invitation into a life of communion with God and with others.

God is Father. Jesus spoke of God with great intimacy. He prayed to God as "Abba" Father. This biblical term *Abba* is an intimate title of affection. It is something like our term "Daddy." This was not the traditional way of talking to God. In fact, in Jesus' day, speaking of God in this way was shocking and scandalous. Jesus not only spoke to God this way himself, but he taught his disciples to pray, "Our Father, which art in heaven. . . ." thus indicating that we can have an intimate relationship with God, similar to that of a child with its father.

I'm afraid some of the significance of this is often lost on us. In Jesus day "Father" did not signify a cold, distant authority figure. Not at all. In Jesus' day "Father" was a term that suggested closeness, intimacy, and affection. In Jesus' day, the father was the one responsible for the raising of the boys in the family. Often the sons learned the trade of their father. Thus, there was a close bond of companionship and affection between father and son. Jesus taught his disciples that they could have this same kind of relationship with God.

This experience of closeness and intimacy with God is the vital center of Christian experience. In Romans 8:15 we are told that we can know God as "Abba" Father. This experience of intimacy with God is called the "witness of the Spirit." We can know we are God's children. We can know we are saved and forgiven. Knowing God in this way is one of the great privileges of Christian believers.

As Father, we think of God as the one who set the plan of salvation in motion: "For God so loved the world that he gave his one and only Son, that whoever believes in him shall not perish but have eternal life" (John 3:16). As Father, we think of God as the one who runs to meet the prodigal son and welcomes him back into the family. As Father, we think of God as the one to whom we pray.

God is Son.   Jesus Christ is one with God. Jesus came into the world as God in human form. We say that Jesus Christ is the "incarnation of God"—that is, God in human flesh. In John 10:30 Jesus says: "I and the Father are one."

Jesus was more than just a human being. He was the living presence of God in the midst of the human race. He dared to tell people: "Your sins are forgiven" even though everyone knew that only God could forgive sins. He dared to speak God's word and will. His miracles were a proof of his oneness with God. Jesus said in John 14:9, "Anyone who has seen me has seen the Father." The implication is that Jesus is one with God; therefore Jesus is God. We call this concept, "the deity of Christ." In

Colossians 2:9 we read, "In Christ all the fullness of the Deity lives in bodily form." In Hebrews 1:3 we read, "The Son is the radiance of God's glory and the exact representation of his being, sustaining all things by his powerful word."

As the Son, Jesus is the highest and best revelation of the nature, purpose, and will of God. Jesus is God revealing himself to the world. In Jesus, we know the heart of God. But he did not simply come to reveal God. The life of Jesus was certainly a great moral example and his teachings continue to be treasured by all Christians throughout the world. Yet Jesus didn't come simply to teach and give us an example to follow. Jesus came to provide us with something we couldn't get any other way—a way to get right with God. Jesus came into the world primarily to be the Savior of the world. He came to provide us with a way back to God. In fact, he is *the only way* to God (John 14:6; Acts 4:12).

In John 14:6 Jesus says, "I am the way, the truth and the life. No one comes to the Father except through me." Jesus did not simply say, "I know the way, I know the truth, I know the life." He said, "I am the way, I am the truth, I am the life." Jesus came into the world to give his life for us. He came to offer us the hope of a new beginning by forgiving our sins. Jesus is the mediator between the sinful human race and the God of holiness who created us.

God is the Holy Spirit.   The Holy Spirit is also identified in the Bible as God. Generally speaking, when God is said to do something, God does it through the Spirit. God created the world through the power of the Holy Spirit. We read in Genesis 1:1–2, "In the beginning God created the heavens and the earth. Now the earth was formless and empty, darkness was over the surface of the deep, and the Spirit of God was hovering over the waters."

The Holy Spirit is God at work in our lives. We generally think of the Father and the Son as being in heaven. Jesus taught us to pray to "Our Father which art in heaven." We remember the story of Jesus ascending into the heavens (Acts 1:1–11). But the Holy Spirit is at work here on earth. The Holy Spirit is that member of the Trinity closest to our personal experience. All the Father desires for us, all that Christ died to accomplish on our behalf, becomes a reality in our lives by the power of God's Holy Spirit. In other words, the Holy Spirit is God in operation.

Think of it this way: as a kind of three-step ladder from heaven to Earth. God the Father is in heaven, designing and initiating the plan of salvation. Jesus is God the Son, as mediator, bridging the gap between heaven and Earth. The Holy Spirit is God on earth, working with us and in us to inspire, awaken, free, and transform us.

Thus, we pray in the Spirit through the Son to the Father. The Spirit inspires our prayer. The Son is our Mediator and Savior, who gives us access to the throne of God. The Father is the One to whom we pray. All of the Trinity is involved.

III. Experiencing God

God wants a relationship with everyone. Out of God's great love, Jesus Christ was sent into the world. We are people created in God's image. We are the special objects of God's love. Jesus Christ was sent into the world "not to condemn the world, but to save the world" (John 3:17).

But there is a problem. We have broken God's law, which distances us from God. Because God is holy and just, he desires holiness in us. God has made his will known in the Bible. Yet we continually rebel against God's will and purpose. We often do the very things that bring pain, shame, and unhappiness into our lives—and into the lives of others. God hates sin. Our sin is the source of conflict, pain, and unhappiness. It is human egotism shaking its fist against the will of God. Not only does sin cause us to feel guilty, it also brings us into condemnation before God. The Bible states it this way: "The wages of sin is death" (Romans 6:23). The "wage" that our sin earns is separation from God and condemnation.

But it is God himself who seeks to overcome this problem. Forgiveness, hope and eternal life are offered to us through Jesus

Christ. God sent his Son to be the answer to the problem of our sin. Through Christ we experience forgiveness and life. God sets us right with himself by the death of his Son. In the Bible this is called "justification." To "justify" means to "set right." We are justified by faith in Jesus Christ. We are forgiven of our sins. The past is no longer held against us. We can begin again.

The basis of our experience with God is grace. Grace is God's desire to forgive us in spite of our sin. Grace is God's love reaching out to us. Grace is the only basis for a relationship with God. We cannot have a relationship with God based on our own goodness, our own knowledge, our religious devotion, or our own spirituality. We could never earn God's favor. Our entire relationship with God is based on God's grace. God's love first reaches out to us in Jesus Christ. Out of mercy and grace God forgives us. Out of grace, God receives us as beloved children. The Bible says: "it is by grace you have been saved, through faith—and this not from yourselves, it is the gift of God—not by works, so that no one can boast" (Ephesians 2:8–9).

God wants people to know and serve him. Our devotion, our songs, our service, and our praise bring joy to the heart of God. Our faithfulness brings glory to God's name. However, many Christian people live in a state of conflict and defeat. Christ is part of their lives, but the Spirit of God is not in control. Their own natural human desires, which the Bible sometimes calls "the flesh," are in control. They are not experiencing the joy and freedom God wants for them. They are trying to live the Christian life—to live as Christ lived—in their own strength. This cannot be done. We need the power of God's Holy Spirit to become the people God created us to be. The power of God's Spirit cleanses us from inward sin and sets us free.

How does this happen? It happens when we fully surrender our lives to God. "Therefore, I urge you . . . in view of God's mercy, to offer your bodies as living sacrifices, holy and pleasing to God—this is your spiritual act of worship" (Romans 12:1). The moment when we stop struggling and striving, and yield our lives fully to God is the moment of spiritual victory. As we give our lives more fully to God, we experience more of the power of God's Spirit.

There are many ways that God brings more grace and sufficiency and love into our lives. We are baptized into the church. We read the Bible so that the Spirit of God can speak to us. We worship God. We pray. We share in community with God's people. We receive Holy Communion. We go to special inspirational events and retreats. We meet together in small groups for prayer, spiritual support, and accountability. We study to learn the meaning of our faith. We serve the needs of others, especially the poor and the outcasts. We seek to find ways to share our faith with others. In these and many other ways the work of God's Holy Spirit is strengthened in our lives. These things open us up to the work of God's Spirit.

The Holy Spirit is the creative power of God in us. God can do great things in and through us. Let us not put a limit on the grace and power of God. We may never know what blessings and grace God may have in store for us.

In conclusion, it is important to remember that the Christian belief in God is more than a doctrine. It is a living experience of the reality of God. God has revealed himself to us as Father, Son, and Holy Spirit. These three are mysteriously One. We were created by God; we live and move and have our existence in God; and it is God who changes us into new creatures in Christ. Jesus came to show us the truth of God, to be our way to God, and to restore our relationship with God. The Holy Spirit has come to help us and empower us to live the Christian life and to be fruitful witnesses for Christ.

Questions

1. Is it possible to know God? If yes—How?
2. How many gods are there? How do we know which one is the right one?

3. Does everybody serve the same god? What gods do people serve?
4. What is the Trinity? (Can you prove, from the Bible, that this doctrine is correct?) What Scripture would you use to support your descriptions?
5. Is it important to have a right understanding of God? Why? Can you describe Him?
6. How does God speak to you? Give an example.
7. When you think of God, which attribute comes to mind?

Craig L. Adams   *Pastor of Zion United Methodist Church, Rev. Adams received his M.Div from Asbury Theological Seminary with emphasis in New Testament studies. He and Robin, his wife of 17 years, live with their two children in Ionia, Michigan.*

Chapter 5

Jesus

by J. Chris Schroeder

ore than a famous leader

MGrowing up in the 1950s and 1960s, I placed great importance on fitting into the activities and ideals of my family. Church on Sunday morning was one of those traditions that I accepted as a part of my life; I still have a string of pins for my many years of perfect attendance. In fact, since most of my friends attended church, or at least youth group, I considered this aspect of life as very normal—even American.

In church I heard about Abraham, Moses, and other great leaders of ancient Israel. There were the brave men of old like David and Daniel, whose heroics would often lead me to great fantasies as a child. And then there were the stories about Jesus, that kindly rabbi (whatever that was) who, it seemed, wouldn't hurt a flea. We celebrated Christmas, but that seemed to represent the act of giving (and of course receiving) rather than a person. And Easter seemed to me to be more of a religious tradition that the church celebrated every spring. Again, it seemed to rep-

resent more of an embellished, maybe even mythological, story
of renewed life than an actual historical event.

Courses in college in comparative religions only helped to
confuse the issue of who Jesus was. He and others like Moses,
Confucius, Buddha, and Mohammed were all variations of the
same theme. They were in the right places at the right times for
people who were in need of direction and a cause. Moses to the
Jews and Mohammed to the Arabs. Jesus—well, he seemed to
be more Western, while Confucius represented a more Eastern
philosophy.

That's it! These were all famous leaders who had various ways
of looking at life based on their different philosophies. Take your
pick which one after whom you would like to pattern your life. It
didn't seem to matter whom you followed, or even whether you
selected from a myriad of other national heroes throughout history. At that time in my life, Jesus was just one of many ways to
discover God and his peace.

Up until the middle of the third decade of my life, the Bible
was just another book. It was the book for those who wanted to
model their lives after Jesus, while the Koran was written for
those who preferred Mohammed. Religious books were written
for the religious part of our lives; novels were to entertain; engi-
neering and electronic books were for my career. They all had
their place, and in their own right were important, though I seldom, if ever, read the Bible.

But in my mid twenties I became involved in a Bible study.
This was prompted by my wife, who was bold enough to engage
me in theological dialogues, especially about eternal life. While
she had an assurance that her eternal destiny was heaven, all I
could do was hope for a "welcome" from God. After all, I was a
moral person and quite religious. I sang in the choir and even
served as an usher in our church.

But the more I studied the Bible, the more I came to realize
that the "Jesus" I believed in was not the same as the one de-
picted in Scripture. True, Jesus was an interesting historical fig-

ure, as was Napoleon, Washington, Moses, and Mohammed. But the Bible claimed that Jesus was far more than just a famous religious leader.

Full Equality with the Father

The Bible revealed astounding claims about Jesus. The gospel of John begins with these words, "In the beginning was the Word, and the Word was with God, and the Word was God. . . . All things were made through him, and . . . in him was life. . . . And the Word became flesh and dwelt among us. . ." (John 1:1, 14). It was clear that John's reference to "the Word" was to Jesus himself. The Bible was portraying Jesus, not only as "with God" but "as God" himself. In fact, it also identified Jesus as the one through whom all things were created (cf. Colossians 1:16–17). My belief that Jesus was merely another in a long line of famous religious leaders was beginning to shatter.

This passage in John also points to the fact that Jesus existed even before creation. His pre-existence before his physical birth at Bethlehem is also mentioned in what is likely an early Christian hymn recorded by Paul in Philippians 2:6–7; "Jesus who was in the form of God, did not count his equality with God a thing to be clung to, but . . . [was] born in the likeness of men." At the birth of Jesus, God put on a human body!

Suddenly Christmas took on a new significance to me. The carols I had sung from memory and the old stories of the season that I had practically memorized took on new meaning. From my favorite carol, "O Little Town of Bethlehem," the phrase jumped out at me: "our Lord, Emmanuel." And from the prophet Isaiah I began to understand "a virgin[1] shall conceive and bear a son, and his name shall be called Emmanuel, which means, God with us" (7:14). This is exactly what Matthew said when he told of the birth of Jesus (1:23). Jesus is "God with us"!

What caused this change in my perception? Up until this point in my life I had always understood that to "believe in" something was synonymous with being "aware of" it. But the Bible says that "even the demons believe" (James 2:19), but it does them no good. If there were demons, I certainly believed that they would not be in heaven. So "belief" or "faith" had some deeper significance. To believe in Jesus, I needed to put my trust in him, like a skydiver puts his trust in his parachute and training. Was Jesus worthy of my trust in such a vulnerable way? Could I abandon my life to him?

I wanted to know more. I had understood that Jesus was one of the world's great teachers who often spoke to his disciples about loving God, our neighbors, one another, and even our enemies. I thought of him as a great moral example building up those who were down and out. He was one who offered forgiveness and not condemnation. He was a prophet of peaceful coexistence for people of different viewpoints.

Who did Jesus claim to be? In a controversy with the Jews over Sabbath laws, he made statements referring to God as "My Father" (John 5:17). His listeners knew immediately what he implied when he asserted that he was "the Son" of God (John 5:19). John records the reaction of the Jews who were listening to him, "This is why the Jews sought all the more to kill him, because he . . . called God his own Father, making himself equal with God" (John 5:18). His contemporaries clearly understood the implications of his words.

From a Western way of thinking, the assertion that Jesus is the Son of God didn't seem all that convincing. After all, I am the son of my father. He lives in one location and is older than I. And my son, who is very active athletically, is at home when I am out traveling. All three of us are different. Yet we are all related.

However, in Eastern thought, that is not what is implied when someone claims sonship with another. ". . . the term 'son of . . . ' did not generally imply any subordination, but rather equality and identity of nature. Thus, for Jesus to say, 'I am the Son of God' (John 10:36), was understood by his contemporaries as identifying himself as God; equal with the Father, in an unequaled sense."[2] This would be more like saying today, "I am a Schroeder, with character qualities, intelligence and good looks that belong to the Schroeder line. I'm not a McClain or even a Slattery!"

We can know what God is like because we can see Jesus and his grace and compassion extended to lost and hurting humanity. He had to be fully divine in order that the salvation he offers to us could be fully complete (Colossians 1:19–20; 2:9–10).

At this point in my life, I needed to make a decision. The evidence of Scripture was overwhelming; Jesus was the eternal God who took on a human body. I was faced with a "trilema" about the person of Jesus. He was either

1. a *lunatic*, deceived about his own identity (Who would want to follow such a teacher and example?);
2. a *liar*, purposefully misleading others (What kind of leader would that be?);
3. what he claimed to be—*Lord of life!*

I decided I had to go with option number three. Therefore, I took a simple step of faith and asked Jesus to take over my life, and his word started to become alive to me.

The Perfect Sacrifice for Sin

With my understanding of who Jesus really was came an insight into why Jesus came to earth. Being a moral person I had a difficult time identifying myself as a "sinner" who needed forgiveness. My credentials, especially in the church, seemed impeccable (except, maybe, for pride). But I soon began to realize that sin was not just doing something "naughty," but just doing things my own way (Isaiah 53: 6). Rather than one who would be caught in adultery, I was more like the Pharisees, the people for whom Jesus had the sternest words.

I also came to realize that the penalty for any sin in God's economy is death. Therefore, I deserved death and separation from God because I had sinned. I understood that God doesn't weigh our good and bad deeds on the scales to see whether somehow the good outweighs the bad. Jesus himself said, "You must be perfect as your heavenly Father is perfect" (Matthew 5:48). I may have been pretty good, but I knew I wasn't perfect. So how could I become right with God?

The more I came to understand about Jesus, the more I realized that this was precisely the reason he came. Only he could put me right with God. Jesus was like us in all respects—except one! Jesus never sinned! (Hebrews 4:15) Being without sin, Jesus became the only perfect sacrifice for the sins of the rest of humanity. (According to Scripture, a perfect, unblemished sacrifice was required for the forgiveness of sins.) Because he was perfect Jesus was the only human who never had to die. But out of his great love for us he offered himself up as the sacrifice for our independence. His death on a cross was the substitute for our sins (Hebrews 9:26).

His resurrection from the dead was the Father's approval of his sacrifice and proof of the claims he made about himself. The resurrection is also the guarantee that our sins have been forgiven and that we can enter into an eternal relationship with God through him.

Our Total Sufficiency for Life

Jesus is unique. He is not only fully God but is also fully human. Without diminishing either aspect of his personhood, Jesus is both God and man. Jesus reveals to us what God is like—loving, gracious, and compassionate. But Jesus also is representative of what true humanity was intended to be.

The impact of this truth never gripped me until several years after I had begun my journey down the road of life with Jesus. I had never thought of myself as a very bad person. I was able to control most of my unhealthful appetites. But one appetite grew increasingly troublesome, almost obsessive in its attempt to control my life. I felt desperate and trapped, even enslaved. A friend came and opened Scripture even further to my understanding with a revelation that transformed my life.

I had always understood that when I opened my life to Jesus, he actually came to set up his residence within me. I knew that theoretically, but had not realized it experientially. What I came to see was that Jesus did not want me to try to model my life after his. He wanted to live his life through me as I lived in total dependence upon him. I had come to the end of my own resources in living the Christian life. Jesus seemed to be saying, "Good, now I can live my authentic life through you."

Jesus' life was such a model of this dependency in his sojourn here on earth. Philippians 2:7 helped in my understanding of this truth. Paul talks of Jesus, "who emptied himself, taking the form of a servant."

Much has been debated in theological circles about the meaning of the word "emptied." It doesn't mean that Jesus' humanity subtracted from his divine attributes. Rather, it seems to imply a veiling of his deity. Jesus set aside his glory and gave up his rights of deity. In other words, Jesus chose not to make use of his deity as the representative Man. He chose, instead, to live his life here on earth with the same resources that you and I have.

What made Jesus' life unique, as the true representative Man, was that he chose to live it in total yieldedness to the will of the Father (John 4:34; 5:30; 6:38). This is the key to understanding Jesus' life as an "example." So often I looked at the scriptural record of Jesus and tried to mimic either his actions or his teachings. But his example is that of total trust in the Father. That was when I came to realize that sin was not so much doing naughty things as it was doing my own thing (Isaiah 53:6). And trying to live the Christ-like life had become very much my own thing; trying to live it in my own strength and resources. I failed time and time again. My frustrations grew with each failure. In fact, they grew to the point of wanting to abandon the pastorate and even my family. It was then that I realized that Jesus came not just to "save" me and give me eternal life, but that he actually wanted to *be my very life!*

Jesus' example as the representative Man is that of absolute dependence on the direction and empowering of God. Jesus said, "Apart from me , you can do *nothing*" (John 15:5) Someone once said that "nothing" is a zero with the circle removed. I've discovered that the Christian life is not my trying to live a similar life to that which Jesus lived, but it is Christ living his life through me by the power of his Holy Spirit residing within me (Colossians 1:27). Living the Christian life means trusting in the fact that Christ now desires to live his life from within me.

Conclusion

I am convinced that Jesus is now seated at the right hand of the Father in absolute authority over all of his creation (Ephesians 1:20–21). But he is not loafing away in a rocking chair. He is actively interceding for me and the rest of the world that he loves (Romans 8: 34). He has chosen to bring us alongside himself spiritually (Ephesians 2:6), to support and encourage us in facing the trials of our daily lives. Because he is the one praying, I am convinced that his purposes will be accomplished in and through my life.

Jesus promised that he would come again (John 14:3) and I await his return. His second coming will not be like his first. At first, he came riding a donkey. His return will have him on a white stallion. During his first coming to this earth, we saw him wooing the world through empowering love. However, when he returns for his second coming, it will be to judge those who refused his gracious offer of forgiveness and grace.

In the meantime, he gave these words to his disciples: "Go and make disciples of all nations . . . teaching them to observe all that I have commanded you" (Matthew 28:19–20). I've been called to help fulfill this command by being a missionary in Eastern Europe. Others are called to be pastors. A friend of mine does this in his automotive repair business, and another friend witnesses as a lawyer. All who are a part of his kingdom have the privilege of his empowering in inviting others to join the excitement of life with Jesus!

Why not join with us? There is *victory in Jesus!* His team wins in the end!

Notes

1 The reference to Jesus' virgin birth is a vital truth of orthodox Christianity. The virgin birth affirms Jesus' deity and lineage from God the Father, and his existence before Bethlehem. It also separates his nature from the sinful nature that all other humans inherit from our original father, Adam.
2 J. Oliver Buswell, *A Systematic Theology of the Christian Religion* (Grand Rapids: Zondervan, 1962), 1:105.

Questions

1. Who is Jesus Christ? How can you tell the real Jesus from all the impostors?
2. How is Jesus different from other prophets, teachers, and religious leaders?
3. How would you describe your relationship with Jesus Christ?
4. Have you ever invited Christ into your life? Can you describe how that happened?
5. Why did Jesus come? Did he accomplish his goals?
6. Did Jesus really rise from the dead? How do you know?
7. Where is Jesus now? Do you believe He is coming back someday?

J. Chris Schroeder *Rev. Schroeder trains pastors in the Czech Republic of Slovakia as a missionary with Biblical Education by Extension. He also works with Grace Ministries providing counseling training in Eastern Europe. His wife Carolyn is also active in ministry. She has a busy counseling ministry and a counseling training ministry in Austria and Hungary. They have been married 29 years and live in Budapest, Hungary with their 13-year-old son David, the youngest of their four children. Chris received his M.Div. from Gordon-Conwell Theological Seminary in 1976.*

Chapter 6

The Holy Spirit

by Mark J. Miller

Who is the Holy Spirit?

Ask the average Christian the question, "Who is the Holy Spirit?" and you will most likely receive confusing answers. The Person of the Holy Spirit is often ignored in many Christian circles today. This may be because he is frequently associated with the more spectacular and sometimes controversial spiritual gifts, like speaking in tongues and miraculous healings. People can't control the Holy Spirit, and his presence is often viewed as spooky or something for the mystics and not for normal people to dabble in. However, all Christians need the Holy Spirit, so let's take a closer look at what the Bible has to say about the Holy Spirit.

The Holy Spirit's Identity and Personality

God has chosen to reveal himself to us as three different persons who are both equal and united. We call this revelation the Trinity: Father, Son, and Holy Spirit. The Holy Spirit is the third person of the Trinity. He is not a vague, ghostly shadow or impersonal cosmic life force. The Holy Spirit is equal in every way with God the Father and God the Son. All of the divine attributes are ascribed to him. He has infinite intellect (1 Corinthians 2.9-11), will (1 Corinthians 12:11), power (Luke 1:35), and emotions (Romans 15:30). To speak of God is to speak of Father, Son, and Holy Spirit. To know the One and Only God is to know God in three distinct persons.

To uncover the identity and personhood of the Holy Spirit, we need to read the Scriptures. There we discover that the Spirit is able to do that which only a living person can do. The Spirit reproves (John 16:8), teaches (John 14: 26), helps us to remember the words and teachings of Jesus Christ (John 14:26), speaks to our hearts (Galatians 4:6), prays and makes intercession for us (Romans 8:26), leads people (Galatians 5:18; Romans 8:14), appoints leaders to serve (Acts 13:2), brings about new life in individuals (John 3:6), seals believers for the day of redemption (Ephesians 4:30), baptizes all Christians into the body of Christ (1 Corinthians 12:13), fills believers (Ephesians 5:18), will someday resurrect Christians (Romans 8:11; John 6:63), and guides us into all truth (John 16:13).

A careful study of the Scriptures also reveals that the Holy Spirit is affected as a person by others. That is to say, the Spirit is grieved by human beings who rebel against him (Isaiah 63:10; Ephesians 4:30); the Spirit can be quenched and resisted (1 Thessalonians 5:19); the Spirit can be blasphemed (Matthew 12:31); the Spirit can be lied to (Acts 5:3); the Spirit can be insulted (Hebrews 10:29); and the Spirit can be spoken against (Matthew 12:32). All of these reflect a personal relationship between the Holy Spirit and Christians. Through experience gained by trusting the Spirit for strength, guidance, and instruction, the believer can come to know the Holy Spirit of God on an individual basis as well as in the community of the saints. The Holy Spirit can draw near to the believer as both comforter and companion on a personal level.

The names given to the Holy Spirit in the Scriptures imply personality or personal attributes. The Holy Spirit is called by many names: the Spirit of truth (John 16:13), the Spirit of life (Romans 8:2), the Spirit of Christ (Romans 8:9), the Spirit of God (1 Corinthians 3:16), the Spirit of promise (Ephesians 1:13), and the Spirit of grace (Hebrews 10:29). These inspired names, combined with the language of the Bible clearly reflect the Spirit's personhood.

The personhood of the Holy Spirit can also be shown through the relationship he has with the believer. The Holy Spirit reveals himself to us by the Word of God and Christian experience. This truth opens the door to discussions of the coming and ministry of the Holy Spirit.

The Coming of the Holy Spirit

The first reference to the Holy Spirit is made in Genesis 1:2. As the biblical account unfolds, it becomes evident that the Holy Spirit worked in and through God's chosen people (Genesis 41:38; Exodus 31:3; 35:31). Although the Spirit's influence is noted throughout the Old Testament, he becomes more prominent in the life and ministry of our Lord (Matthew 3:16; Mark 1:10; Luke 3:22). Jesus promised his disciples that a day would come when the Holy Spirit would be available to believers in a new way (John 14:16; Acts 1:8). According to our Lord, the Holy Spirit was to be "poured out" at Pentecost (John 16:13-14). This "pouring out" of the Spirit "upon all people" was prophesied by the Old Testament prophet Joel (2:28–29).

After Jesus ascended into heaven to be at the right hand of the Father, he sent the Holy Spirit as he promised to the disciples. The Holy Spirit came as the "Comforter," "Advocate," "Counselor," and "Helper" (John 14:16–17, 26). The Greek word for *comforter* or *helper* is *paraclete,* meaning the "one called along beside." Therefore, the Holy Spirit is the companion and friend who is called alongside the believer to energize, strengthen, and empower. As Jesus had come to exalt and reveal God the Father, so the Holy Spirit was sent to exalt and glorify God, the Son (John 16:13–14).

The Ministry of the Holy Spirit

As was mentioned earlier, the Holy Spirit is a person, yet with divine characteristics. There are six ministries of the Holy Spirit that need to be looked at in a little greater detail.

(1) The Spirit "convicts the world of sin, and of righteousness, and of judgment" (John 16:8). This ministry of the Holy Spirit is to the whole world. The convicting involves a deep inward conviction and personal sorrow for sin. Perhaps the greatest of sins is in respect to the sin of unbelief. I say this because the ministry of Jesus Christ and the witness of the apostles dealt so strongly with the concept of faith in "[him] who was crucified, and made both Lord and Christ" (Acts 2:36–38; Romans 3:22, 5:1; Galatians 2:16). Christ suffered in our place; we were bought with a price; and we are now God's children (1 Peter 2:21; Romans 8:16; 9:8). But the unbelieving world must also be warned that it is sinful and will be judged for it.

(2) The Spirit regenerates and brings spiritual transformation (John 3:6). By the regenerating power of the Holy Spirit, the one who has faith in Christ passes immediately from the law of sin and death to the law of the Spirit of life (Romans 8:2). Believers are made partakers of the divine nature (2 Peter 1:4), and Christ has given them eternal life (Titus 3:7). The divine nature is a nature of holiness and righteousness. The Spirit therefore sanctifies (sets apart as holy) the believer to the extent that the believer turns his or her life and will over to him.

(3) The Spirit indwells or lives in the believer (Romans 8:9; 1 Corinthians 2:12; 6:17). This indwelling is an intimate presence that can be lovingly and powerfully acknowledged or grievously and selfishly ignored (Isaiah 63:10; Ephesians 4:30). The Scriptures promise that we are united with Christ, ". . . you in

me, and I in you" (John 14:20). We exchange our weakness for his strength, our sinfulness for his holiness, our defeat for his victory. The more we allow the Holy Spirit to guide us, the more we shall love and serve the Lord Jesus Christ. Day by day we will be more conscious of his loving and abiding presence. The Holy Spirit's help, guidance and benefits are as close as a heartbeat or as far away as we push him.

(4) The Spirit baptizes all Christians into the body of Christ (1 Corinthians 12:13). Not only does the Holy Spirit live in each believer, but the believer can be so vitally joined to the Lord by the baptism with the Spirit (1 Corinthians 6:17; Galatians 3:27) that the believer is said to be "in Christ." To be "in Christ" is to be joined to Christ. The believer, like a branch that will soon die when it is cut off from its source of life, is now grafted into the true vine, Jesus Christ. The believer is now divinely made a part of Christ's body, the church.

(5) The Spirit seals believers for the day of redemption (Ephesians 4:30). The presence of the Holy Spirit in the believer is proof of divine ownership and security that can be denied only by the believer's own rejection and falling away (Hebrews 6:4–6). The Spirit of God and of Christ will never "leave us or forsake us" and "will be with us always" (Deuteronomy 31:6; Matthew 28:20), if we do not totally turn away from our faith in Jesus in apostasy and sin (Hebrews 6:4–6).

(6) The Spirit fills believers (Ephesians 5:18). There is a once-for-all indwelling presence of the Spirit given to Christians through faith. Although there is one giving of the Spirit to the believer through faith and rebirth, there are many fillings. Someone once said that with the filling of the Holy Spirit we do not really acquire more of the Spirit of God so much as the Holy Spirit acquires more of us. It is a surrender to the Spirit that becomes more and more a continuous "state of being," if we so allow.

When we are filled with the Holy Spirit we are, in essence, filled with Jesus Christ. A power much greater than our own is released within us and through us for service to God. Every Christian is to be filled with the Holy Spirit in order to have the power to be a more effective witness for Christ. Before his ascension into heaven, Jesus said, "But you shall receive power when the Holy Spirit has come upon you; and you shall be my witnesses both in Jerusalem, and in all Judea and Samaria, and even to the remotest part of the earth" (Acts 1:8). In fact, every biblical reference related to the filling of the Holy Spirit is related to power for service and witness to God.

The Gifts of the Holy Spirit

All true Christians are members of the body of Christ (1 Corinthians 12). The Apostle Paul tells us that as various parts of the human body have different functions, so various parts of the body of Christ will have different spiritual gifts and responsibilities. Again, this is possible only through the power and guidance of the Holy Spirit.

Spiritual gifts come in many different forms to different people. The Spirit of Christ gives gifts to people, like apostles, prophets, evangelists, pastors, and teachers to "prepare God's people for works of service, so that the body of Christ might be built up until we all reach unity in the faith and in the knowledge of the Son of God and become mature, attaining the whole measure of the fullness of Christ" (Ephesians 4: 11–13).

The Spirit of God gives gifts to people: "There are different kinds of gifts, but the same Spirit. There are different kinds of service, but the same Lord. There are different kinds of working, but the same God works all of them in all men. . . . to each one the manifestation of the Spirit is given for the common good" (1 Corinthians 12: 4–7). Various gifts listed in the Scriptures are the message of wisdom, the message of knowledge, faith, gifts of healing, miraculous powers, prophecy, distinguishing between spirits, speaking in different kinds of tongues, and the interpretation of tongues. Although the gifts of God are virtually endless, all of these mentioned are at work by the one Spirit of God who gives to each person as he determines (1 Corinthians 12: 8–11). Every Christian must leave the assignment of the gifts, and the manner in which they are revealed, to the Holy Spirit. However, we are told to "eagerly desire spiritual gifts" (1 Corinthians 12:31) and to pray for certain gifts (1 Corinthians 14:12). The "sign gifts" (Mark 16:17–18), as they are often called, are not necessary or exhibited by all. (As it has been said, "You don't have to, but sometimes you get to!") But in the same respect, every Christian should remain open to all the ways the Holy Spirit gives his gifts to reveal his presence. It is also prudent to note that any or all of the gifts of the Holy Spirit will profit little unless we are motivated by love (1 Corinthians 13). However, if we are open to the Spirit of Christ, we will have the love of Christ shed abroad in our hearts (Romans 5:5).

The Fruit of the Holy Spirit

Along with the gifts of the Spirit, Christians filled with the Spirit will exhibit fruit in their lives. The fruit of the Spirit is love, joy, peace, patience, kindness, goodness, gentleness, self-control, and faithfulness (Galatians 5:22–23). The fruit of the Spirit seems to have more to do with everyday life that reflects something of the character of God. Thus, the Spirit's fruit is the Christian's godly character. The text in Galatians 5 seems to indicate that there is a struggle within every believer whether to allow the Holy Spirit to have his way. In short, that means there is always a choice the believer must make.

Though the fruit of the Spirit is reflected in the transformed character of each believer, spiritual gifts are for the common good of the church, the body of Christ. There is no reason for pride in the heart of a Christian because of the fruit of the Spirit or spiritual gift given by God. This is what troubled the Corinthian church and it can get us into trouble as well. No Christian should belittle another's gift.

The Christian's Response to the Holy Spirit

The personal response to the saving presence of the Holy Spirit is to be one of praise and thanksgiving. The overall response to the filling of the Holy Spirit varies from person to person. Some may experience a calm assurance and quiet realization of a greater faith in Christ and the promises of his word (John 14:16). To others, the response to the Holy Spirit may be a more emotional and/or physical experience not at all unlike that which the disciples experienced on the day of Pentecost, and at other times (Acts 2:4, 10:46, 19:6; 1 Corinthians 12:10, 14:5).

The Holy Spirit in My Life

Before I was called by God to the ministry, I remember my own doubt concerning the strangeness of much that is associated with the Bible's teaching on the Holy Spirit. Many people I knew were opening themselves up to the Holy Spirit and many wonderful but somewhat startling things were happening. Staunchly conservative friends and long-time United Methodists were suddenly speaking or praying in tongues, being miraculously healed, and given supernatural understanding and discernment. I was skeptical about this new emphasis on the Holy Spirit until my own wife prayerfully asked for the filling of the Holy Spirit of God and started praying in tongues. Those new Spirit-filled believers even began to display more of the fruit of the Spirit in their lives.

Seeing all this, I wanted to experience it myself. After several days of prayer with my pastor and with other Christian friends, it seemed that God was not hearing my prayers. After one night of seeking the Lord, it was not until I was alone in my car, frustrated and again in prayer, that suddenly a tremendous feeling of warmth and assurance overcame me. It suddenly occurred to me that in my heart I had actually been *demanding* of the Holy Spirit of God a specific sign or gift to prove everything that I had seen in others, rather than honestly seeking the filling of his Holy Spirit.

I decided to confess that selfish sin and ask for nothing except to be totally Christ's, to be his servant, and to be filled with his Spirit. Then, with the warmth, came strange but prayerful utterings from my mouth. I wept at the hearing of them.

Many times since, but especially in my ministry, I have seen God work miracles (physical, emotional, and spiritual) in the lives of others because of an opening up to the filling of his Holy Spirit. I could recount story after story, and all because my pastor was faithful to God and the Scriptures in challenging us to open ourselves up to all God had for us in the filling of his Holy Spirit.

The most important thing to remember is that the Christian should submit to an authentic response of the Spirit's moving. Preconceived "proper or improper" responses to the Spirit hinder him and show more of our will at work than God's. The end result of our real and varied responses to the Holy Spirit is a special desire, ability, or power to give witness to Jesus Christ in the world.

There are a few essentials to remember when seeking the filling of the Holy Spirit. The Scriptures tell us that all sin should be confessed (1 John 1:9); that the whole life, body and soul, be surrendered to him (Romans 6:13; 12:1; 1 Thessalonians 5:19); that the believer ask for the Spirit in faith, believing that the Spirit will be given (Luke 11:13); and that there be a moment by moment reliance upon the Spirit (Galatians 5:16).

In Summary

Beginning in Old Testament times, and especially on the day of Pentecost and continuing through the centuries, the work of God has always been accomplished through those who were both led by and filled with the Holy Spirit. The Holy Spirit helped Abraham, Moses, Esther, Ruth, Paul, Peter, Mary, Martha, the apostles, and all the believers in the early church. In more recent times the Holy Spirit has helped Martin Luther, St. Augustine, Martin Luther King, Jr., Billy Graham, Pat Robertson, Charles Colson, and millions of other believers. Both men and women can accomplish great things for God's kingdom *if* they submit to the Holy Spirit.

The Holy Spirit already indwells every born-again believer. But *indwelling* and *filling* are not always the same experience. While every Christian is indwelt by the Holy Spirit, we are also commanded by Scripture to be filled with the Holy Spirit (Ephesians 5:18). The Greek in this passage literally means "be filled continually" or "keep on being filled," which indicates that many fillings are not only possible but expected. In that passage in Ephesians, Paul was talking to Christians, not unbelievers. Therefore, the Christian who is not filled with the Holy Spirit is being disobedient to God. It is sad but true that Jesus is far more eager to fill us with the Holy Spirit than we are to be filled. The main roadblock to being filled with the Holy Spirit is our own will. Our will is made weak by a lack of knowledge of God's Word, fear, pride, secret sin, worldly mindedness, and a lack of trust in God. Why not stop right now and ask God to fill you with the Holy Spirit?

Questions

1. Who is the Holy Spirit?
2. What did the Holy Spirit come to accomplish?
3. How were the disciples different after having an experience with the Holy Spirit?
4. Why does the Bible say we need to ask for the Holy Spirit (Luke 11:13)?
5. Take a close look at Acts 19:1–7 and then answer the following questions:
    a. Why did Paul ask—"Did you receive the Holy Spirit when you believed?" How would you answer that question?
    b. How did Paul describe John's baptism? What does that mean?
    c. How did the men respond to Paul (19:5)?
    d. What happened (19:6)? Can that happen today? If yes— has it happened in your life?

6. What difference has the Holy Spirit made in your life?
7. How is the Holy Spirit working in the life of your church?

Mark J. Miller   *An Elder who has served local United Methodist Churches for 13 years, Rev. Miller had a varied work background prior to entering the ministry, including stints as a service and sales representative and an over-the-road truck driver. He graduated* magna cum laude *from the University of Indianapolis 11 years after he graduated from high school. He received his M.Div. from Garrett Evangelical Theological Seminary with emphasis in Pastoral Care. He and Linda, his wife of 19 years, have two teenagers and live in Lawrenceburg, Indiana.*

Chapter 7

Salvation

by David A. Seamands

Back in the 1700s, a British ship was caught in a storm that was so furious it seemed all aboard would be lost. The terrified captain began to cry out to God to save him in spite of his sins and wicked life. Not only was he a slave trader, but he was also personally enslaved to a life of lustful involvement with the slaves. God heard that prayer of Captain John Newton and changed his life. In response to his experience of deliverance, he wrote the gospel song that has become a favorite throughout the world.

> Amazing grace! How sweet the sound
> That saved a wretch like me!
> I once was lost, but now am found;
> Was blind but now I see!

John Newton's experience is often referred to as "salvation." Does that word turn you off? If so, it's because we don't understand its true meaning. One of today's favorite TV programs is *Rescue 911*. It's an amazing collection of true incidents in which

people are rescued (saved) from life-threatening situations because someone called 911 for help. If we gave that program a
biblical name, we might call it "Salvation 911." The Bible is
filled with stories of God's loving grace, which delivers and saves
from guilt and the power of sin.

God rescues people from not just the obvious, open sins like
those of a John Newton, but also the self-righteous sins of the
deeply religious, like a John Wesley. Mr. Wesley was an ordained
clergyman who was sent overseas as a missionary to America.
Yet in spite of being pious, prayerful, and disciplined, he found
it difficult to live with the guilt he felt. He lived without the peace
or joy that he believed should accompany someone serving God.
Then one night at a prayer meeting on Aldersgate Street in Lon-
don, England, John Wesley found what he had been looking for.
In his own, now famous words, "I felt my heart strangely warmed.
I felt I did trust in Christ, Christ alone for salvation: and an assurance was given me that he had taken away my sins. . . ." That
was the experience from which came the Methodist Church. It
did not begin when a bad man became a good man, but when a
good man became a Christian!

Let us look at the most important biblical teachings regard-
ing salvation and what they mean for our practical everyday living. Then we, too, will have something to sing about.

To understand the full value of salvation it might help to start
by asking a few questions. Who needs it? From what are we saved?
Just what is the deliverance that salvation promises us? First and
foremost, the Bible declares that all have sinned (Romans 3:23).
Therefore, we are saved from sin and our lost state of being right
with God. Matthew 1:20-25 tells of an angel sent with special
instructions for the naming of Jesus, "because he will save his
people from their sins." And Jesus plainly said he had come "to
seek and to save what was lost" (Luke 19:10). Salvation rescues
us from a way that will lead to destruction and the loss of our
souls. It offers us an abundant life eternal. We cannot do this by
and for ourselves, no matter how sincerely we determine to "try

harder." Only the saving power of Christ can "break the power of canceled sin and set the prisoner free."

Three Important Facts

(1) Salvation is a divine gift and not a human achievement.

It can't be earned or acquired by our performance, no matter how religious or perfect that might be. ". . . [I]t is by grace you have been saved, through faith— and this not from yourselves, it is the gift of God" (Ephesians 2:8). Yes, even the faith to believe is God's gift. "So that no one can boast" (Ephesians 2:9). God wants every person to be saved (1 Timothy 2:4), and it is his mercy and patience alone that makes this possible (2 Peter 3:15).

During the Napoleaonic Wars, a young, battle-weary French soldier fell asleep while on guard duty. He was court-martialed and sentenced to die. But he was the sole supporter of a widowed mother who somehow arranged an audience with the emperor himself. Falling prostrate at Napoleon's feet she begged him to spare her son's life. Finally, weary of her pleas, he said coldly, "But madam, your son does not deserve mercy. He deserves to die." To which the mother immediately replied, "Of course, Sire, but if he deserved it then it wouldn't be mercy, would it?" We are told that Napoleon was so touched by her response that he pardoned her son. Yes, salvation is undeserved, unmerited, unearnable, and unrepayable—the free gift of God's grace unrelated to our worthiness.

(2) Jesus Christ, in his life, death, and resurrection is central to our salvation.

The very reason Christ came into the world was not "to condemn" it (John 3:17) but "to save sinners" (1 Timothy 1:15). So Scripture declares, "There is salvation in no one else, for there is no other name under heaven given among mortals by which we must be saved" (Acts 4:12, NRSV). Thus, Jesus is the "pioneer," "the trailblazer," and the "source" of our salvation (Hebrews 2:10; 5:9). At the heart of it all is the "message of the cross" where

"Christ died for our sins and was raised again for our justification" (Romans 4:25). Though this may sound like "foolishness,"
it is really the "power of God for salvation to everyone who has
faith" (1 Corinthians 1:18; Romans 1:16).

(3) Salvation always involves repentance.

Repentance is more than remorse, feeling sorry for our sins.
Repentance is the result of a "godly sorrow" for our sins, which
gives us both the desire and the power to turn away from them. This,
combined with faith, involves taking God at his word and trusting
in his gracious offer of mercy. In this sense, we are saved from all
that would ruin our souls in this life and in the life to come.

Three Aspects of Our Salvation

(1) Along with rescuing us *from,* salvation also restores us *to* a new relationship with God.

We call this "justification." This is more than pardon or ac-
quittal for our sins, it reconciles us with God. We are now "in
Christ" and therefore are a "new creature; the old has gone, the
new has come! All this is from God who has reconciled us to
himself through Christ . . . [for] God was in Christ reconciling
the world to himself, not counting their trespasses against
them . . ." (2 Corinthians 5:17–19). Such New Testament descriptions of salvation are like invitations to sing the doxology. No
wonder Charles Wesley begins so many hymns with the simple,
exultant, joyful word, "O," as in, "O for a Thousand Tongues to
Sing!" Salvation is something to get excited about.

Furthermore, whether the awareness of this salvation comes
to us gradually (as a process) or suddenly (as a crisis) we can
know it with certainty, because God's Spirit is bearing witness
with our spirits that we are children of God (Romans 8:15).

(2) There is also a continuing, present-tense aspect to salvation.

Often the word is used as meaning "being saved." We call
this "sanctification," the process whereby the Holy Spirit makes

us more and more like Christ in our inner attitudes and outer actions. In John 14–16, Jesus makes it clear that the chief work of the Holy Spirit is to reproduce his character within us and his ministry through us. 2 Corinthians 3:18 describes this process as "being transformed into his likeness with ever-increasing glory."

(3) Our ultimate salvation, which lies in the future, we call "glorification."

We can experience salvation and enjoy it here and now, but its full consummation will come to us only in the world to come. That is when Jesus Christ is enthroned King of all kings and when "every knee shall bow and every tongue confess that Jesus Christ is Lord" (Phillipians 2:10–11). At this point, salvation will include deliverance from every sin, mistake, and handicap; every physical, emotional, and spiritual imperfection; every separation, sorrow, and even death itself. An incredible scene and song shall take place. Though indescribable and dazzling, its theme will still be salvation. Charles Wesley puts it into lyrical praise in the third stanza of his great hymn "Ye Servants of God," which is taken from Revelation 7:9–12:

> "Salvation to God, who sits on the throne!"
> Let all cry aloud and honor the Son:
> The praises of Jesus the angels proclaim,
> Fall down on their faces and worship the Lamb.

The Place for Good Works

We are saved for more than a right relationship with God and the resulting good feelings of assurance; we are saved for good works (Ephesians 2:10). As John says it (1:12; 3:7), we have been "born" into God's family. Paul describes it as "adopted into" (Ephesians 1:5; Romans 8:15–17; Galatians 4:5–7). Therefore, we are no longer servants trying to earn God's approval or achieve salvation by our performance. We are now God's "children" who want to perform good works out of gratitude for the gift of salvation.

It is a wonderful thing to experience God's gift of salvation. Have you experienced it?

It begins by asking God for it.

Questions

1. What does it mean to be saved?
2. What are we saved from?
3. Who saves us and why?
4. Is everyone saved? Will everyone be saved in the end? Prove your position from the Bible.
5. Does God want everyone to experience salvation?
6. What are the three aspects of salvation?
7. Have you experienced salvation? Why not tell your story to your group.

David A. Seamands   Born in India of missionary parents, Rev. Seamands is a graduate of Asbury College, Drew Theological Seminary, and holds a Master's Degree from the Hartford Seminary Foundation and honorary doctoral degrees from both Asbury College and Asbury Theological Seminary. He and his wife Helen served as United Methodist missionaries in India for 16 years. For 22 years he was senior pastor of the Wilmore United Methodist Church and for 8 years was Professor of Pastoral Ministries at Asbury Theological Seminary. David and Helen Seamands have been pioneers in the Marriage Enrichment and Engaged Discovery movements. They have three children and nine grandchildren. Now retired and living in Nokomis, Florida, he continues to speak, write, and conduct seminars on emotional and spiritual wholeness. His books have sold over one and a half million copies and have been translated into 21 languages. They include Healing for Damaged Emotions, Putting Away Childish Things, Healing of Memories, *and* God's Blueprint for Living.

Chapter 8

People

by Joy J. Moore

Who am I?
"IN THE BEGINNING GOD CREATED . . ."
So begins the book that holds the designation of being God's Word. The story that tells his-story, and our story.
Who am I?

The Bible is not a book of fairy tales. It is not the myths of a masculine being. The Bible is the manufacturer's handbook, containing the message that answers the age-old question "Who am I?" Rather than a list of replacement parts for the million-dollar body or an instruction manual of cultural options, Scripture is the textbook for living in God's world, on God's terms. If we are to live successfully, a biblical education is essential for understanding humanity. The Bible is the truth that transforms existence into life.

Any attempt to comprehend the mystery of human identity is dependent on acknowledging the intricate link between a divine creator and the spiritual hunger so evident in human striving.

Such discussions must be rooted in understanding that through faith in Jesus we are "the people of God."

Though a gymnast may know her abilities, her enthusiasm is often directly related to knowing whether her team is favored to win or lose. How she trains is dependent not only on her teammates but on the coach, the facilities, and the expectations of everyone involved. Who she is, as victorious and capable, is linked to whose uniform she wears. Knowing *who* we are proposes a mutual consideration of *whose* we are.

The Image of God

Humans are more than merely created beings, for we uniquely bear the likeness of the Creator. To begin to unpack this bewildering controversy, we must recognize that every morning, when a person looks in the mirror, a miracle is seen. For God consecrated a lump of clay when humankind was stamped with the birthmark "made in the image of God." The reflection staring back with crusty eyelids, and matted hair, is the handiwork of God. However, on any given day we may not like the reflection in the mirror. But we don't paint the mirror with make-up or pin a power suit to the reflection. We change clothes, fix our hair, brush our teeth, and do whatever else is necessary to change the image so that it reflects what we hope to see. In a similar way, God wants to change us. While we were made in the image of God, that image was distorted by sin. As we view that distorted image of human frailty, we will not correct the reflection by simply studying the image. It can be restored only through faith in Jesus Christ. In order to glimpse the perfection we are to strive toward, we must seek God first. Because we bear the autograph of God, it is only by knowing God that we will come to understand ourselves. Both individual and collective self-understanding will come only when we focus on the majesty of God.

The matchless God, stepped out of nowhere and created somewhere. The almighty God, encountered nothing and it became

something. The compassionate God took nobody and made somebody. It is to this powerful Creator that we owe our existence and
our understanding of ourselves.

The Bible declares that we are made in the "image of God."
Yet we continue to struggle with how that likeness translates to
fragile mortals. Where do we bear the image of God? That question has baffled scholars throughout the ages and still remains a
mystery. However, I believe that the image of God in us is best
described by our attitudes and actions. Dr. Martin Luther King,
Jr., called it the "content of our character." The character of God
is love, for the Bible declares "God is love" (1 John 4:8). That
love is reflected in God's attitude and action.

God's attitude is one of love. God's love is not a response to
what we do, but God's choice to be in relationship with us. God
has found in each of us something lovable. Therefore, God reaches
out to us even when we run the other way. Yet in spite of our
rejection of God's love, the hound of heaven doesn't give up.
God has chosen to love us, in spite of our negligence to believe
and receive. When God finds us we are drawn by an overwhelming sense of love into the presence of the Holy Spirit.

Our Self Image

In spite of our failure to love unreservedly, we have been loved
unconditionally. In spite of our inability to trust, either ourselves
or others, we have not only been trusted to reflect God's image,
but entrusted with proclaiming God's truth. In response to this,
we can count ourselves as victorious. Part of that victory involves
a healthful self-image of viewing ourselves as God views us.

As humans, we continually strive for self-understanding. This
generation, not unlike any other, has both chosen to reject God's
self-revelation as a bridge to our potential and been convinced
that we can be "godlike" on our own. Our rejection of God's
design leaves us in a continual search for meaning.

When we observe the consequences of living without a scriptural self-image, we see ourselves as victims and have a tendency to blame everyone else for our problems. Psychology tells us we can't erase the patterns of pathological lies passed on to us from our families of origin. Psychiatry says we can't change our patterns of behavior. Sociology suggests that we will never be free of the patterns of addictions to drugs, nicotine, alcohol, sex, power, or victimization. Science sees the patterns, but says we can't plant seeds of transformation, remove the stones of segregation, crack the rocks of religiosity, dig out of the dungeons of despair, cure the disease of racism, or survive the stench of individualism. And theologians often don't know how to respond.

We have been convinced that we are not responsible or even capable of alternative responses. By laying the blame on others, we act as if we have no ability to make decisions, choose our actions, or live proactive lives. Yet one of the gifts of God is the freedom of choice. Living on God's terms is not just going through the rituals of religion, but reflecting the image of God by the way we live and the decisions we make.

It is silly to blame God for human irresponsibility. When we fail to choose to live as children of God, we find ourselves victims of circumstances. Regardless of what psychology observes, psychiatry analyses, sociology strategizes, science discovers, or theologians think, God reveals a pattern of living that "takes a licking but keeps on ticking." By calling for a community of people who view the world from a biblical perspective, God summons a society of countercultural citizens who attempt actively to promote a lifestyle of integrity and purity.

The Revelation of Jesus Christ

When we seek God, it is important for us to remember that God has revealed himself to us most clearly in Jesus Christ. When the distorted image comes face to face with the original likeness of God, in Jesus Christ, we recognize the malformations. This identification transforms our striving from seeking temporal pleasure, to desiring eternal reconciliation. We become willing to choose to be accountable to the community of others who are also in such a relationship with God. We must recognize our abilities and limitations. All of us are born in sin. Our "first birth" makes us children of Adam and Eve, which means we are children of disobedience. Our human nature causes us to seek our will over, and often against, God's will. No amount of education, religion, or discipline can change the old nature; we must receive a new nature from God, by placing our trust in Jesus Christ. When that happens, there is a restoration of the original nature of God within us.

Created to Be in Relationship

By donating dignity to the dirt of creation, God not only designed human form but human function. It is God's design for us to need each other. In all of creation, it is recorded only once that God said, "It is not good." That moment was when God looked upon Adam, and declared ". . . it is not good for man to be alone" (Genesis 2:18). Then God created woman and decreed that we would be a people in relationship, a people in community. Marriage is not a social suggestion or a civil contract but a divine design. God coupled man and woman by joining together two distinct beings and described unity as the choice of harmony.

It was God's idea that marriage would be male and female. It was God's idea that family exists as the union of one man and one woman for life, blessing that union with commonly conceived children. It was such a good idea that an attempt to counterfeit this gift with other options has been offered. People today venture to recreate the recipe for family without the basic ingredients. Blended families, homosexual covenants, serial marriage after divorce, and living together without the benefit of marriage are all forgeries in the creation of the community called family.

The Judeo-Christian story of humanity names people by family, not by job, age, or race. God distinguishes everyone by whose we are. Today, family is almost obsolete. Race, gender, and sexual activity are more important than whose child or sibling you are.

It is more important to talk about whether we live in America or Asia than if our fathers are the same race. Think about it. Would race mean as much if we identified ourselves by our ancestors instead of our outward appearance?

Our eyes have become clouded by a racist/sexist agenda that is a mask of the evil that has blinded our society for centuries. We allow social theories, psychological antidotes, and theological gymnastics to redefine the spiritual wickedness that undermines our ability to witness that we all bear the image of God. Too quickly we cry "ism" without naming sin, sin. Too often we seek justice without reconciliation.

We cannot correct this evil by legislation, protest, or policy. Only the forgiveness of our sins will renew this society. Don't get killed fighting the wrong battle. We need the integrity that is a result of a consistent walk and talk, a faithful witness to Jesus Christ, a relevant articulation of the Word of God and a patient listening to the hurts, angers, and opinions of others. To quote Dr. Tony Evans, "White is only right when it agrees with Holy Writ and Black is only beautiful when it's biblical."

People of the Word

The most frequently quoted Bible verse is John 3:16—"For God so loved the world that he gave his only Son, that whoever believes in him should not perish, but have eternal life." It is evident from that verse that God does not just love one race, but all people of every race in the variety of colors genetically engineered by the Creator. *All* have been created by God with value and worth. Jesus did not die on a cross for only a certain group of people who were born in the right country, to the right parents, in the upper economic brackets. God loves *all* the world. Our worth is measured by God's decree.

It appears that we have forgotten what humanity means. Sociologists seek equal opportunity. Psychologists celebrate freedom of choice. Advocates attempt accessibility. Governments guarantee defense. Organizers offer civil rights. Theologians try pluralism. Historians reinterpret reality. Scientists suggest genetic inequality. If we believe that this generation has done the best at being fully human, then why have those who bear the identity "made in the image of God" demonstrated a limited capacity to reflect the God whose name is Love?

The people of God view the world through the lens of Scripture, taking seriously the mandate of identification by confession of faith rather than the complexion of one's face. The people of God define themselves first as those who believe that God's self-revelation was in the incarnation of Jesus of Nazareth. The people of God recognize that the God who spoke everything into being from nothing also offers eternal life through the crucified Jesus, who rose bodily from the dead.

The Community of Faith

Our lives have been changed because we have a solution for a sin-sick world of increasing complexity. The people of God come together, not simply to explore religion, but to tell a story that cannot be told anywhere else. We gather in this community to experience God in Jesus Christ. We are different because we view the world differently. Our questions have been answered. We don't always understand the answers, but we trust in the God who gives them. Like them or not, we believe they are sufficient for living right before God through the power of the Holy Spirit.

When reading the Bible, we remember that God's love and God's power come to us because of God's grace. The truth of our identity is not a reward for our diligent searching. It comes by God's grace to show us a new way that we not only didn't want to know but didn't want to take—a way called "community" that fixes the limits of our identity at the point of naming Jesus Christ as the Son of God, Savior of the world and Lord of all. We make such a claim, not on our own wisdom, but by the grace of God who chose to reveal the divine nature through the Word, and invited us to accept the Holy Spirit's power to live as God's people—a people whose story is created by God, edited by Jesus

Christ and empowered by the Holy Spirit.

Like the athlete of a winning team, we are now favored for victory. We train by *the* Book. God has placed before us a standard of moral integrity, loving character, and self-denying discipline. The expectations are high, but the victory is sure when we trust in Christ.

Questions

1. What does it mean to be created in God's image?
2. How was that image distorted? Has that affected everyone?
3. Is it possible to restore that image? Explain your answer.
4. Is racism evil? Why or why not?
5. Why do people matter to God?
6. Have you ever sinned against God? How would you know if you had?
7. Is there any hope for people today? Why or why not?

Joy J. Moore   A middle-school mathematics teacher by training, Rev. Moore has developed and led seminars on biblical worldviews, racial reconciliation, African American experiences, communication styles, contemporary values and Christian Women Encouragement. She has served as a pastor in the West Michigan Annual Conference since 1988 and was the first African American female ordained an elder in that conference. She is currently on staff at Asbury Theological Seminary in Wilmore, Kentucky. She received her M.Div. from Garrett-Evangelical Theological Seminary.

Chapter 9

Holiness

by David L. Flagel

Bill has been a Christian for only a few months. When he first discovered the love of Christ, his life was filled with a deep and profound joy. He thought his problems were over until he found himself yielding to the same old temptations as before. Did that mean his initial experience of salvation was not genuine?

Jean has been a Christian for many years. Long ago she came to grips with the fact that she still has a lingering capacity for saying thoughtless, unkind things to people she cares most about. Invariably she regrets her words later, after the damage has been done. If her faith is genuine why does she continue to be so unloving?

What both Bill and Jean fail to realize is that salvation does not end with confessing Jesus Christ as one's personal Savior. As important as that initial act of faith is, it is only a beginning. Perhaps you've seen the poster that says, "Be patient! God isn't finished with me yet!" The doctrine of holiness is the teaching that God isn't finished with us once we become Christians. Not by a long shot! There is much more he wants to do in us and for us (1 Corinthians 2:9).

John Wesley used a vivid word picture to describe salvation when he said that salvation is like entering a house. Stepping onto the porch of the house is sorrow for sin and a desire to walk in a new direction (repentance); walking through the front door is receiving forgiveness of sins and a new relationship with God (justification); dwelling within the house is learning to live a life of holiness to the Lord (sanctification or holiness). In effect, he was saying that one can no more consider salvation complete at justification than one can fully live in a house without ever going further than the front door. Christian holiness is learning to live in the Lord's house, a life that pleases him and brings him glory.

Sadly few ideas are more unwelcome in the society in which we live than the idea that a person must be holy. Yet the Bible says without it no one will see the Lord (Hebrews 12:14). As Tony Evans writes in *Our God Is Awesome,* "After God has cleaned you up, he will fix you up so that he can use you up." The "fixing-up" is God working to make us holy in heart and life.

What Is Holiness?

One way to understand the meaning of holiness is to consider the family of biblical words related to it. New Testament words like "sanctify" and "saint" are derived from the root word for "holy." With slight variations among them, the basic meaning of these terms, as they are used in the New Testament, involves being set apart to belong to God by faith in Jesus Christ (1 Corinthians 6:19,20). But holiness is also a process by which, in cooperation with and by the power of the Spirit of God, we submit our lives more fully to God, day by day (James 4:7). Living a holy life involves exhibiting more of the character of God in our spirit, soul, and body. It is the fruit of the Spirit finding expression in daily life (Galatians 5:22–23). Holiness, Wesley taught, is loving the Lord with all our being and our neighbor as ourselves. Holiness is not sinless perfection; it is rather love "emanating from a sincere heart."

Because holiness is so easily misunderstood, let me expand upon several basic truths that might help to clarify our understanding.

First, Christian holiness is not absolute holiness. Only God is absolutely and perfectly holy. When Moses and the people of Israel fled from Pharaoh's army they miraculously escaped through the Red Sea. Afterwards, they paused to worship God and they sang in joyous praise "Who among the gods is like you, O Lord? Who is like you—majestic in holiness, awesome in glory, working wonders?" (Exodus 15:11) They had just witnessed several spiritual battles between God and the gods of Egypt, and they rightly concluded that no one is like the Lord. He alone is majestic in holiness. You and I affirm this truth when we sing: "Only thou art holy; there is none beside thee, / Perfect in power, in love and purity." Only God is absolutely and perfectly holy.

Wait a minute, I can hear you say. If that is true, if only God is holy, then how can we talk about Christian holiness? Since only God is perfect and therefore holy, isn't the term "Christian holiness" a contradiction?

The answer is "no" and the reason lies in the grace of God. Just as God's undeserved favor has rescued us from the penalty our sins deserve, so his favor bestows the gift of holiness. You see, Christian holiness is dependent holiness. You and I depend upon God to give us new life in Christ, and we can depend upon him to make us holy. The moon shines in the night sky, though it has no light of its own. It reflects the light of the sun. So we Christians are to reflect the holiness of God, though we have no holiness of our own. That is why it is called "Christian" holiness to distinguish it from the absolute and perfect holiness of God.

Second, Christian holiness is God's will for *all* his people. Holiness is not reserved for "super saints" nor is it limited to "full-time" Christians like pastors and missionaries. God's will is that all his people be holy.

That God desires a holy people is clearly spelled out in the Bible. Peter declares: "But just as he who called you is holy, so be holy in all you do; for it is written: 'Be holy, because I am holy'" (Peter 1:16). The writer of Hebrews, speaking about the role of godly discipline in the believer's life, says, "Our fathers disciplined us for a little while as they thought best; but God disciplines us for our good, that we may share in his holiness" (12:10). And Paul, writing about the glory of the Church says, ". . . Christ loved the church and gave himself up for her to make her holy, cleansing her by the washing with water through the word, and to present her to himself as a radiant church, without stain or wrinkle or any other blemish, but holy and blameless" (Ephesians 5:25–27).

These Scriptures (and many more besides) clearly teach that holiness is God's will for all his people. Indeed, the entire story of the Bible from Genesis to Revelation can be viewed as the story of a holy God seeking to create a holy people. And if God desires something, you and I can be sure he will bring it to pass!

Third, Christian holiness is both already and not yet. Perhaps you've noticed the apparent contradiction in Paul's letters to the church at Corinth. On the one hand, he talks to them as if they are already holy Christians when he says, "To the church of God in Corinth, to those sanctified [remember the root is "holy"] in Christ Jesus" (1 Corinthians 1:2). Again, in 2 Corinthians 1:1 Paul addresses them as "saints" (again the root word is "holy"). On the other hand, the Corinthian believers were shockingly unholy, and Paul found much to criticize (for example, drunkenness at the Lord's table, selfishness at the potluck dinners, partisanship, and even toleration of incest within the church). The question begs to be asked, "How can a people, the Corinthian believers, be both holy and unholy?" Another example of this apparent contradiction is found in Hebrews 10. In verse 10, the writer says, "We have been made holy through the sacrifice of the body of Jesus Christ once for all." Yet in verse 14 he says, "Because by one sacrifice he has made perfect forever those who are being made holy." How can this be? How can it be that the recipients of the letter to the Hebrews can be considered to "have been made holy" and at the same time still be in the process of "being made holy"?

The answer lies in the fact that Christian holiness is both already and not yet. Through faith in Christ, God declares us already "holy." Some call this "positional holiness." Thus, through the grace of God, in Christ, the Corinthians were sanctified and made saints of God even though they still needed to grow in their experience of Christian holiness (cf. 2 Peter 3:18).

It's like this. When my three children were born they were complete and perfect in body and mind. Yet even though they were complete and perfect at birth, they still needed to grow and to develop into the persons God created them to be.

The moment we believe we are already made holy by faith in God's Son, Jesus Christ. Yet the extent to which we must still grow and develop in our relationships with Christ, as Paul says "being conformed to the image of his Son" (Romans 8:29; 2 Corinthians 3:18), we are not yet complete in holiness. Therefore, Christian holiness is both an already and a not yet.

Fourth, Christian holiness is our spirit cooperating with God's Spirit to make us more like Jesus. We come now to the core of Christian holiness: Christlikeness. This is the "not yet" element of Christian holiness toward which we are growing. When first we accept the Good News of Jesus Christ, the Holy Spirit takes up residence within our lives. He dwells within us as Jesus promised (John 14:16–17). But the Holy Spirit wants to do more than dwell within us. He wants to rule and reign over us. He wants to go from simply being "resident" within our lives, to being "president" over our lives. The more he rules, the more our lives become Christlike.

What Is the Key to Growing in Christian Holiness?

Perhaps the key word in this fourth statement is the word "cooperate." God will not force himself upon us, either before

we believe or after. He desires our willing and loving cooperation with his plan for us. We've already seen that this plan involves holiness of heart and life. The question is whether we will
cooperate with the Holy Spirit as he molds and shapes us into the
likeness of Christ.

One cannot overestimate the importance desire plays in growing in Christian holiness. We must want to have more of God in
our lives before we will ever see it happen. This desire or longing
for God has its source and its power in the Holy Spirit. As someone has said, however, our "wanter" must match our "needer"
before we'll begin to desire Christian holiness.

A couple of years ago I was in the midst of a particularly dry
season in my Christian life. As a pastor and as a Christian, I was
defeated and discouraged. The joy of the Lord was not my
strength. I had no strength or joy. While attending a minister's
Conference at Asbury Theological Seminary the Holy Spirit began to work in my heart in a fresh way. I'll never forget it. We
were gathered in the gymnasium for a time of worship. The song
leader was leading us in several praise choruses, when suddenly,
and without warning, tears began to stream down my face. I realized in a fresh, new way my need for Jesus and my utter dependence upon him. My heart overflowed with praise and gratitude
to God for his many mercies as I began to want more of Jesus in
a way I hadn't for a long time. The words to an ancient Irish
hymn became especially precious to me during those days and
have remained so to this day. They express the desire so important to growing in Christian holiness:

> Be thou my Vision, O Lord of my heart;
> Naught be all else to me, save that Thou art;
> Thou my best thought, by day or by night,
> Waking or sleeping, thy presence my light.

The Scriptures are filled with examples of men and women
desiring God. As Paul said about his own experience, he had not
fully arrived, but by God's grace he pressed on to make

Christlikeness his own (Philippians 3:12–14). This desire finds expression best in the book of Psalms. "Create in me a pure heart, O God, and renew a steadfast spirit within me" (51:10), and "give me an undivided heart, that I may fear your name" (86:11). Psalm 42 says, "As the deer pants for streams of water, so my soul pants for you, O God. My soul thirsts for God, for the living God" (verses 1–2). This kind of desire for God has its source in the Holy Spirit and is the seedbed for a life of growing in Christian holiness.

What About You?

I've tried to show what Christian holiness is and is not, though it is best seen not in words but in flesh and blood. Of course, the clearest and best example is the life of our Lord. In the final analysis, Christian holiness is Christlikeness. God's intention for each of us is that we grow to become more like Jesus (Romans 8:29).

What about you? Do you desire more of Jesus Christ? Do you long to know him better and be filled more with his Spirit? May the Holy Spirit light a flame of desire within each of us that will blaze to the glory of God.

Questions

1. Define holiness.
2. Is it possible to live a holy life? Is it possible to grow in holiness? Why?
3. How do we live a holy life?
4. Is holy living boring? Why or why not?
5. Can you name some biblical characters who lived holy lives?
6. Do you know anyone alive today who seems to be living a holy life? What makes you think so?
7. Are you living a holy life? Is there room for improvement in your life? If yes, how?

David L. Flagel   *Pastor of LeValley and Berlin Center United Methodist Churches, Rev. Flagel is a member of the Good News Board of Directors. Good News is a renewal movement within the United Methodist Church. He received his M.Div from Asbury Theological Seminary. He and Rebecca, his wife of 24 years, live in Ionia, Michigan where they homeschool the youngest of their three children.*

Chapter 10

Eternity

by Wade S. Panse

People have a great interest in time. Human history is measured in increments of eras, ages, and generations. Human government is marked by rule, reign, and term of office. Human environment is monitored by seasonal change, tidal movement, lunar and solar positions. Human life is celebrated by days, months, and years. Every human activity, whether industry, communication, or athletics, finds its success metered by hours, minutes, and seconds. Ask "What time is it?" and you are sure to have a listening ear. Human beings want to know about time.

Ironically, as much as we know about the measurement and management of time, there is no greater mystery to the human understanding of time than that of eternity—time without end. It is a paradox that while eternity challenges the intellect and stretches the imagination, it tends to shrink the experience and perspective of life. Therefore, it is no surprise that eternity often remains the subject of academic discussion and the object of artistic expression but seldom is the topic of neighborly or family conversation. To speak of eternity is to be reminded of finitude, mortality, limitation, and restriction.

Remarkably, the Bible, which records for us the activity of God, is astonishingly clear and accurate in describing where, in the measurement of time, God is at work. For example, through the millennia of recorded biblical history, the reader is able to mark time with such statements as:

"In the year that King Uzziah died, I saw the Lord" (Isaiah 6:1).

"The word of the Lord came to him in the thirteenth year of the reign of Josiah, son of Amon, King of Judah" (Jeremiah 1:2) .

"On the fifth of the month, the fifth year of the exile of King Jehoiachin, the word of the Lord came to Ezekiel the priest" (Ezekiel 1:2).

"In those days, Caesar Augustus issued a decree that a census should be taken of the entire Roman world. This was the first census that took place while Quirinius was governor of Syria" (Luke 2:1–2).

The Arena of God's Activity

Any serious reader of Scripture quickly discovers, however, that biblical writing is no mere chronology of divine, human, or historical events. Instead, such historical markings become the touchstones of time, leading the reader to a larger and longer understanding of life. Eternity, in all its mystery, is revealed as the arena of God's activity. Note, for example, Hebrews 11, the great faith chapter that scrolls through time lifting, for the reader's attention, the numerous persons of biblical history who model the life of faith. Their lives reveal the activity of God.

If God is at work in the arena of eternity, then that is the arena in which we are given life and encounter God. (*Note:*

Because God is eternal and has no beginning and no end, it may be argued that God does not operate or perform in the arena of eternity, but God *is* eternity. It is here to be understood that God is eternal, and is not limited or restricted by any description of time.)

Humans and Eternity

In contrast to the eternal nature of God—who was, who is, and who forever more shall be—human beings have no eternal past, but do have a life on earth and an eternal future. Humans have not always existed. At conception we have our beginning and our introduction into the eternal arena of God's activity. This existence will be interrupted by death (abortion, fatal accident, terminal illness, suicide, murder, etc.), but our existence, from the moment of conception, will be without end.

This understanding of life's origin and eternal existence explains the reason for the sincere emotion and urgent activity surrounding the right-to-life advocates and abortion opponents so active in our culture today. The Christian doctrine of eternity has important social and political relevance for our contemporary world. Among the essential truths of the Christian faith, the doctrine of eternity must be understood with clarity and conviction . With all its relevance and application to present life situations, eternity cannot be relegated to abstract theological discussions as some nondescript "pie in the sky, by and by" concept. Instead, an articulate and accurate doctrinal understanding of eternity should light a fire of holy activity within the Christian church and in the life of every Christian. It is with such doctrinal conviction about the importance of eternity that missionaries suffer hardship and endure the loneliness of family separations. It is with such doctrinal conviction that evangelists persist in their preaching without the security of pastoral appointment. It is with such doctrinal conviction that the young mother finds the courage to petition Congress or parade in protest outside an abortion clinic.

And it is with such doctrinal conviction that the local church is moved from the apathy of cloistered worship to the dynamic of social service, evangelistic zeal, and missionary fervor.

Eternal Questions

During our life on earth the question must be asked, "How will I spend eternity?" Not to ask this question is to assume a most fatalistic and depressing position: that this life—this existence in this time and place—is all there is. How small and insignificant this leaves human life when placed against the measure of eternity! If this is true, then we are quite literally next to nothing in our existence, and without purpose in our living.

The Christian faith holds forth another response. This earthly life is not all there is and we are not without purpose in it. We are created in the image of God, and by design have the characteristic of eternal existence. So it is by God's design, power, and initiative that humans are created for eternal existence with God.

Until the fall of creation through sin, recorded in Genesis 3, eternal existence was ideal. The created individuals experienced love, joy, fellowship, and life in great abundance and intimacy with God and with one another. Life was eternal, and eternity was life in the will and plan of God. There was no other existence known but that of peace with God forever.

But when sin came on the scene, it interrupted the ideal, fouled the fellowship, and killed the life that had its origin in the love of God. Life was lost in quality, but not quantity. Eternal existence persisted, but outside the will and presence of God. Such existence, bereft of Divine presence, is biblically described as eternal punishment because it perpetuates the penalty of sin—namely, separation from God. It is this unending existence of perpetual punishment that Jesus speaks of as hell (Matthew 23:33) and against which the Church shall always prevail (Matthew 16:18).

It may be said that in the continuum of time without end, there are two tracks of eternal existence. There is the track of eternal punishment, traveled by those who persist in living outside the will and purpose of God, and there is the track of eternal life, which is the way of the redeemed. There is the road to hell, and there is the way to heaven.

The good news of the Christian faith, and the gracious gift of Jesus Christ, is eternal life!

Jesus said to the disciples, "I am the way and the truth and the life. No one comes to the Father except through me" (John 14:6).

Hope for Eternity

By faith, the Christian accepts Jesus Christ as the atonement for sin and the Savior of the world. With sins forgiven, therefore, the believer is the recipient of eternal life, not eternal punishment, through Jesus Christ. Heaven is the eternal reward of the Christian, not hell.

The perceptive reader understands that eternal life, as the gift of God to those who believe in Jesus Christ, begins at the moment of belief, not the moment of death: ". . . whoever believes in him [Jesus] shall not perish but have eternal life" (John 3:16).

Consider the impact on the believer of this eternal truth:

■ The terminally ill patient is not shattered by the fear of death but instead has the confidence of life's victory over the grave through Jesus Christ. Life eternal is already being lived.

■ The grieving parent has "a peace that passes understanding" knowing that the dead child rests in the arms of almighty God. Life does not end at the grave.

■ The young Christian convert exudes confidence and joy because sin has been forgiven and life forever with Christ has just begun. Eternal life begins with belief in Jesus Christ.

We are all interested in both time and eternity. It is the conviction of the Christian, however, that all persons live in the realm of eternal time. By the grace of God, may each of us come to know the poetic and prophetic word that "the LORD . . . will watch over your life; the LORD will watch over your coming and going both now and forevermore" (Psalm 121:7–8).

Eternity is not just doctrine. It is life.

Questions

1. How long is eternity? When does it begin?
2. According to the Bible, what happens when people die? Does everyone die?
3. What determines where a person will spend eternity?
4. What do you think about the possibility of reincarnation? Does the Bible teach reincarnation?
5. Can you describe what the Bible says about heaven?
6. Have you come to the place in your spiritual journey where you know for sure that when you die you will go to heaven? If yes, how did you discover that assurance?
7. How would you respond if you were asked this question: "Why should God let you into heaven?"

Wade S. Panse *Rev. Panse is Senior Minister at St. Joseph First United Methodist Church. He is Director of Alumni for Asbury Theological Seminary and received his M.Div. from that institution. He is also a trained and experienced mediator. He and Patricia, his wife of 28 years, live in St. Joseph, Michigan. They have four grown children.*

Chapter 11

Satan

by Den Slattery

Many Americans in the last half of the twentieth century have struggled with the idea of a real devil. Yet in the last few years there have been so many reported cases of satanic rituals throughout the country that it is difficult even for skeptics to continue to deny that there is something evil in our world. Not everyone would agree to name that evil force "Satan," but few would argue against the idea of something evil controlling certain people. When the question is asked, "Why is there so much evil in the world?" it is important to note that much of the evil we see on this planet, in one way or another, comes from Satan. He is the embodiment of evil. Therefore, *believing in a real devil helps life make more sense.* Trying to explain war, violence, and perversions of every sort becomes difficult to understand, if Satan is left out of the equation. It is clear from the Bible that Satan is our enemy who looks for ways to trip us up (1 Peter 5:8). Yet because of the victory that Jesus won on the cross we don't need to fear. But we should have some understanding of his strategies for future reference. They just might come in handy.

One note of caution: Two dangers face us when dealing with this subject; the first is to think that Satan is everywhere at all times (he is a created being with limitations); the second danger is to act as if he doesn't exist (the Bible speaks of him from Genesis to Revelation). In this chapter I hope to present a balanced view.

Personal Testimony

There was a time when I served Satan. It started when I was only six years old and came in contact with gypsies who taught me how to be a fortune teller. For the next eighteen years, I ventured further into the world of the occult by using ouija boards, horoscopes, magic, hypnosis, ESP, and eventually even casting spells on people. I saw amazing things happen through my occult activities, enough to know that I really was tapping into some kind of power. I was tricked into thinking that it was my own power that created what I commanded. It wasn't until I was 24 that I discovered how Satan had deceived me. The power I had encountered was simply an introduction into Satan's magic kingdom, which he used to gain control over my life. It took Jesus Christ to set me free. The power of Jesus is greater than Satan's.

What Can We Know About Satan?

Satan is not God, nor is he equal with God. Satan is a created being who is the exact opposite of God. God is good; Satan is evil. God is light; Satan is darkness. God is all powerful; Satan has limited power. God knows everything; Satan has limited knowledge. However, in spite of his limitations, Satan has a bad habit of trying to imitate God. He does this by going to the opposite extreme. Since human life is sacred to God, Satan wants humans killed. God wants people to obey him; Satan wants people to rebel against God. God desires that people worship him; Satan wants people to worship anything but God. God wants people to walk in the light and be holy; Satan wants people to walk in darkness and be unholy. In almost every way, Satan tries to copy what God does, only in reverse. This compulsion goes all the way down to the smallest details, such as the color of candles for worship. For example, God's people use white candles; Satan's followers use black.

Names of Satan

The Bible uses many different names for Satan, each of which describe some aspect of his character. Among these names are the tempter (Matthew 4:3), the deceiver (Revelation 12:9), the accuser (Revelation 12:10), the god of this age (2 Corinthians 4:4), the prince of the power of the air (Ephesians 2:2), the father of lies (John 8:44), the serpent (Revelation 12:9), the destroyer (Revelation 9:11), prince of the devils (Matthew 9:34), a murderer (John 8:44), angel of light (2 Corinthians 11:14), and the dragon (Revelation 12:9). The Bible also gives us some insight into how he operates. He is crafty (2 Corinthians 11:3), slanderous (Job 1:9), fierce (Luke 8:29), deceitful (2 Corinthians 11:14), powerful (Ephesians 2:2), conceited (1 Timothy 3:6), and cowardly (James 4:7). Jesus indicated that Satan's agenda is to "steal and kill and destroy" (John 10:10).

Origin of Satan

Satan was created as a powerful angel who eventually fell into sin because of his pride (Ezekiel 28 and Isaiah 14). The bib–lical record indicates that he wanted to be like God, so he started a rebellion involving one-third of all the angels (Revelation 12:7–9). This rebellion led to his expulsion from heaven along with the other rebellious angels who sided with him. Those rebellious angels are the demons we hear so much about in the Gospels. To this day Satan roams across the earth looking for trouble.

Satan's Final Destination

There is no truth to the claim of many Hollywood movies that Satan currently lives in hell and enjoys every minute of it.

The Bible indicates that he currently lives on the earth with freedom to roam around as he looks for opportunities to cause havoc and destruction. At some time in the future, the devil will be thrown into the lake of fire where he will be tormented forever and ever (Revelation 20:10). Thus, the flames of hell will be his final destination, but hell is not his current home.

What Can the Devil Do?

In the book of Job we find some revealing things about human suffering and the devil. Job was a servant of God who seemed to do everything right. Satan requested God's permission to test Job's true character (Job 1). God said okay. The hedge of God's protection dropped and Satan did his evil work of destruction. Job's servants were slain and his animals were stolen by the invading armies of Sabeans; fire from heaven fell on another group of Job's servants, killing both the men and sheep; Chaldeans attacked the camel herds, killing servants and stealing the animals; a violent wind storm ripped apart the house where all of Job's children were gathered, leaving only one survivor. In chapter 2, Satan struck Job with painful boils from head to foot and seems to have been instrumental in sending three of Job's friends to condemn him. Even Job's wife seemed to be inspired by the devil when she said to him, at his lowest moment, "Curse God and die!" (v. 9) That was exactly what Satan wanted Job to do. From this story we can conclude that Satan has in his arsenal: limited power over nature, disease, war, demons, people, signs in the sky and miracles on the earth. He uses his power to afflict pain, suffering, death, discouragement, and bitterness on human beings, whom he hates.

Satan's Encounters with Humans

The first two people to encounter Satan were Adam and Eve in the Garden of Eden. Genesis 3 tells the story of their downfall. In essence, Satan told Eve, "You can't believe what God says. If you listen to me you'll be just like God. I can make you wise, if you'll follow my advice." Satan communicated with Eve in such a way that she began to think his thoughts. He still attacks people with thoughts like little darts that prick the mind (Ephesians 6:16).

Eve was tempted by the devil in three areas: *lust of the flesh, lust of the eyes,* and *the pride of life* (Genesis 3:1–6; 1 John 2:26). Satan still uses those three areas to tempt people today. It is interesting to note that the new-age craze now teaches the same lie that Satan told Eve in the Garden of Eden, "You can be a god (like god)." Furthermore, it should be noted that when Jesus was tempted in the wilderness (Matthew 4), he was tempted by the devil in the same three areas as was Eve: lust of the flesh ("Turn the stones into bread to satisfy your hunger"); lust of the eyes ("I'll give you everything you can see"); pride ("If you are the Son of God, jump and prove it"). Jesus defeated the devil by using the written Word of God. "It is written . . ." All three times he quoted from the book of Deuteronomy.

Again we see Satan communicating with his victim, indicating that he uses words or thoughts to tempt. Jesus used the Words of God to defeat him, giving us an example to follow.

The Demise of Satan

It was said of Jesus that he came "doing good and healing all who were under the power of the devil" (Acts 10:38). To reveal that authority and power, Jesus went everywhere healing the sick, cleansing lepers, raising the dead, and casting out demons. Today Satan tries to get us to rebel, hate, kill, sin, and perform every perversion that we can imagine. By contrast, Jesus told people to repent, submit to God's will, to love, forgive, and sin no more. Jesus defeated Satan in every encounter they had, from infancy to the cross. Jesus never gave in to the temptation to sin, even though he was tempted in every way that we are (Hebrews 4:15). Strangely enough, his ultimate victory came by allowing Satan to influence people to kill him on the cross. However, what appeared to be defeat turned out to be the greatest victory when Jesus rose from the dead three days later. Colossians 2:14–15 describes it this way, "He forgave us all our sins, having canceled the written code, with its regulations, that was against us and that stood opposed to us; he took it away, nailing it to the cross. And having disarmed the powers and authorities, he made a public spectacle of them, triumphing over them by the cross."

What Can Demons Do?

Satan is still in the rebellion business. His helpers are called demons or evil spirits. Usually, when a person engages in spiritual warfare it is with one of the devil's representatives and not the devil himself. Satan isn't like God who can be everywhere at the same time. Therefore, he sends his helpers to do his dirty work. The Scriptures indicate that there is a system of rank in Satan's army: principalities, rulers, powers, and evil spirits in high places (Ephesians 6:12). Daniel had a revelation on this issue when he was visited by an angel of God. The angel said, "Since the first day that you set your mind to gain understanding and to humble yourself before your God, your words were heard, and I have come in response to them. But the prince of the Persian kingdom resisted me twenty-one days. Then Michael, one of the chief princes, came to help me . . ." (Daniel 10:12—13). It is interesting to note that the prince of the Persian kingdom (an evil spirit) was able to hinder God's message from getting to Daniel until an angel of similar power (Michael) came to assist in the battle. It seems reasonable to assume, therefore, that there must be similar battles raging in heavenly realms over all the other countries of the world. Some demons work to control cities, while others work on individuals.

Demonic Attacks

I have frequently witnessed the activity of demons working in individuals. And I have also witnessed the power of the Holy Spirit to set the demonized free in the name and authority of Jesus Christ. Evidence of demonic activity in an individual is sometimes difficult to nail down because it can often involve things that, in some cases, seem to have other causes. Some of those might include sickness (Luke 13:11–16), bizarre behavior (Mark 5:1–20), epilepsy (Mark 1:21–27), blindness (Matthew 12:22), deafness (Mark 9:14–29), difficulty speaking (Luke 11:14–15), and a host of other problems. However, it is clear from Scripture that demons can and in fact do inflict humans with various problems that can appear as physical, emotional, or mental illnesses. In those cases, the cure is to cast the demons out in the name of Jesus Christ.

Defeating Satan Today

It is clear from Scripture that the victory of Jesus has been passed on to all who are his followers. However, that victory has to be enforced. That is why we are told to pray (Philippians 4:6), resist the devil (James 4:7), control our thoughts (2 Corinthians 10:5), not to give in to anger (Ephesians 4:26–27), and to put on the whole armor of God (Ephesians 6). We are told to do those things because God wants us to be like Jesus and not like Satan. The very fact that in the Lord's Prayer Jesus taught us to pray, "Deliver us from the evil one" (Matthew 6:13), should be enough to convince us that this battle is real. We are at war with Satan and his army who threaten to destroy anyone who gets in their way. While many people feel the only safe haven from this battle is the church building, I assure you, after having served in many different churches over the years, that the church building is not the place of refuge some seem to think it is. I am convinced that many of the petty church fights that happen in every church, of every denomination, are the work of Satan. When a fight breaks out in the local church, the work of the church is hindered, people feel betrayed, and often they feel compelled to leave that local assembly. The result is that their witness to the community is destroyed by a gossip war that burns like a forest fire. The church is not exempt from Satan's attacks.

Another tactic of Satan is to try to trick people to uphold his agenda by appealing to their personal weaknesses. Behind most forms of perversion, envy, greed, drunkenness, hatred, violence, murder, witchcraft, pride, lust, rebellion, idol worship, homo-sexual practice, abortion, deception, every sin, and occult activity the devil and his army of demons are in some way involved. They are, at the very least, near by applauding the activity. Many people have fallen into his traps. Like a wolf that tries to separate an animal from the rest of the flock, so Satan often looks for opportunities to get us away from other believers. The Bible describes him as a roaring lion looking for his next victim. Could it be you?

There are several steps we can take that will help us to be victorious over the evil one:

1. Spend time daily reading the Bible and praying; it would help to memorize key Bible passages (Psalm 119).
2. Put on the whole armor of God through prayer and with faith (Ephesians 6).
3. Get together with other Christians frequently (Hebrews 10:25).
4. Obey God. Do what God says, not what the devil says (John 14:21).
5. Reach out to others by witnessing to them and serving them (Mark 16:15 and Matthew 5:16).
6. Overcome evil with good (Romans 12:21).
7. Gain control over your thought life (2 Corinthians 10:5).

Conclusion

Satan is tricky. He often appears to people as a friend or an angel of light who comes to offer help (2 Corinthians 11:14). Dealing with him can be like trying to catch fog; he often slips right through our fingers. But Jesus has given us the authority and the tools to deal with the devil. Those tools are outlined for us in Ephesians 6 as the armor of God. They include the Bible, the shield of faith, the helmet of salvation, the breastplate of righteousness, prayer, and the gospel. Revelation 12:11 indicates that our victory over the devil is won by the blood of the Lamb, the word of our testimony, and self-denial. First John 5:4 includes faith as a necessary ingredient for victory.

God has also given us the freedom of choice. We don't have to do what the devil wants us to do. Satan has often been likened to a dog on a long chain. Satan can do only so much. He can't force us to do things against our will, unless we are living in rebellion against God and have yielded to evil spirits who exert some control over our will. But the devil never has total control or power over people unless they give it to him. It is important to remember that the devil is only an angel. He may be powerful and cunning, but he is not God. He didn't create the world, but is a limited being who can do only so much. It is evident from the Scriptures that he can't even control his own destiny (Revelation 20:1–10). His final destination will be the flames of hell. We should keep that important fact in mind.

I doubt that people can live for very long before they have an encounter with some representative of Satan's army. That's why he is called the god of this world; this is his turf. The more we yield to him, the more control he has over our lives. The Bible tells us to resist him and follow Jesus. Let us examine our lives to see who is in control. Are our lives bringing honor and glory to God because of our faith, love, and good deeds? Or are our lives helping the devil's kingdom as evidenced by our sin, rebellion, and evil works? Jesus said we can know the difference by the fruit we see in people's lives. Let's live in such a way that Jesus is glorified and his kingdom expanded.

Finally, be careful. We have a cunning enemy who is invisible but very present. In Christ we have the victory over him. However, we need to enforce that victory through use of the promises of God's Word.

Questions

1. How do we know if there really is a devil? Are demons real?
2. Describe what the Bible says about Satan.

3. Why does the devil cause trouble? How do you think he feels about you?
4. What is the devil capable of doing? Does he have any limitations?
5. What are some of the names the Bible gives to Satan? Why are they important?
6. What are some subtle ways in which Satan seeks to influence us?
7. How did Jesus resist Satan?

Den Slattery   *A Pastor and Army Chaplain, Rev. Slattery served in a special Marine C.A.P. Unit in Vietnam from 1969–1970 and in the Army, (Avionics) from 1971–1975 with tours in both Vietnam and Korea. He received his M.Div. from Anderson University, with emphasis on Pastoral Ministry, and is just completing his D.Min., with emphasis on Church Growth, from Trinity Evangelical Divinity School. In 1996 he was awarded the Denman Evangelism Award by the West Michigan Conference in conjunction with the Foundation of Evangelism. He and Karen, his wife of 17 years, live in Marcellus, Michigan, where they are homeschooling their four children. He is the author of* From the Point to the Cross *and several articles and tracts.*

Chapter 12

Church

by Gregg Parris

J esus said, "I will build my church; and the gates of hell shall not prevail against it" (Matthew 16:18, KJV). This rich promise reminds us that the church of Jesus Christ is the most dynamic, powerful, and transforming influence in our world. It is the church that will ultimately triumph in Jesus Christ! With Jesus as our head, builder and cornerstone, we are being formed as living stones into a significant temple of worship and ministry.

Certainly we are living in some of the most dramatic days in all of church history. The current impact of the gospel around the world is breathtaking. It is estimated that 70,000 people are coming to faith in Christ every day. Those new Christians are helping to plant as many as 45,000 churches every year. Since 1900 the number of Christians in both Africa and South Korea has grown to encompass 40% of the population of those countries. During that same time period, the Christian population of Latin America has grown to more than 40 million people. China has experienced a great upsurge in the number of Christians, even though they are persecuted daily. It seems obvious that the unreached people in the world have never received a more loving, passionate, and prayerful invitation to receive the new life found in Jesus Christ.

However, while God is doing a remarkable work across the globe, the North American church is in transition. Mainline denominations in North America are declining in virtually every measurable way. The United Methodist Church, for example, has lost almost four million members in the last three decades. The median age of members in United Methodist churches also continues to climb, indicating that, as a denomination, it is dying of old age. Our influence seems to wane as we drift further and further from our theological, historical, and traditional moorings. In general, the church in America is not experiencing the spontaneous work of the Holy Spirit that many others seem to enjoy in various parts of the world. Some have described our society as post-Christian because our values, standards, and morals continue to unravel. One thing is clear, in spite of rapid church growth worldwide, we are living in a culture that is increasingly antagonistic toward Christianity.

Therefore, as the body of Christ, we must adjust our thinking. We must discipline ourselves to look differently at the way we do business. Our perspective on how we are perceived by the world and the way we function must change. The church is no longer viewed as the little chapel on the corner where people come to be fed. It is more and more perceived as an irrelevant option in an already busy week. We must make adjustments. The extent of our willingness to make these adjustments will directly affect our ability to fulfill God's destiny for our generation. Keep in mind, while the message of the gospel of Jesus Christ is sacred, the methods of advancing the gospel are not. While an uncompromising commitment to the timeless truths of the Christian faith should be embraced, we need to continue to seek the Holy Spirit's wisdom on how to do the work of the kingdom. We desire to move forward with sober, prayerful determination to discern the voice of the Holy Spirit and respond to him in faithful obedience.

The Union Chapel Story

In 1981 Union Chapel United Methodist Church was a small (70 in worship attendance) rural church in the cornfields of east central Indiana. It was my first appointment out of Asbury Theological Seminary; it included Union Chapel and a smaller church five miles to the north. A few weeks into my tenure, three elderly women approached me after a Sunday morning worship service. Opal, Gladys, and Floccie respectfully and confidently announced to me that they had been meeting together on a regular basis for over 30 years to pray for spiritual renewal in their church. This was my first real indication that God might have some unusual plans for that small church.

Later that autumn, it seemed good to a few of us to conduct a week-long series of meetings to stimulate spiritual life in the church and the surrounding community. The idea was met with no small degree of resistance and skepticism. We did, however, see about 25 persons attend each of the first four nights of special meetings. We sang all the right hymns, "Revive Us Again," "Victory in Jesus," "Power in the Blood," etc. There was good preaching from a friend of mine and always an invitation at the conclusion of each service for people to respond to Christ in a personal way. Our hymn of invitation was "Just As I Am," and we sang all 36 verses while everyone remained just the way he and she had always been.

On Thursday night the meeting followed a similar course. We came to the appropriate conclusion, and I prepared to pronounce the benediction. At this point our organist of 31 years stood to her feet and asked to speak to everyone. She stood next to the upright piano and while looking at the empty altar rail began to reminisce about the past. She recounted occasions when people would actually seek God at the altar of this church. She paused, then began to suggest that one of the reasons others had not sought God at the church altar was because she had not been faithful to do so. She then confessed her own sins of apathy, indifference, and lukewarmness. As her sins were confessed, she began to weep. Her voice choked with emotion as tears welled up in her eyes and began to spill down her face. When she was no longer able to speak, she bowed her head and began to sob. Her shoulders heaved as tears of repentance flowed. It was a holy moment. It was also painful, provocative, and convicting. Many found their way to the altar that night and made fresh commitments of their lives to God.

The news of that night spread quickly in our rural community. The following Sunday morning our normal worship attendance of 70 expanded to 145. In that service 21 persons made personal decisions to make Jesus Christ Savior and Lord of their lives for the first time. The church was experiencing the early indications that God was answering the prayers of Opal, Gladys, and Floccie.

Two years later we held our last service in the original building with more than 300 in attendance. For the next four years, we met in a local high school auditorium, climbing in attendance to more than 700. We then renovated a car dealership and relocated 12 miles from our original building. Today we use the auto showroom as our sanctuary, which we affectionately call "the showroom of heaven." Our current worship attendance exceeds 1,200 per Sunday. I speak of the numbers to indicate the great work God accomplished in the hearts and lives of many precious people. To God be the glory!

Church in Community

Two basic issues must define the church in these later years of the twentieth century. First, we must be the church in *community.* Community refers to the people of God in **authentic relationships.** The Bible is clear: the church is a fellowship, a family, a body, a flock. God has intentionally designed us to need one another. Fellowship is not what a church does, but what a church is. The church is to operate on the basis of relationships. It is in the context of community that people experience the nurture, support, encouragement, and accountability they need for successful Christian living.

Community is enhanced by *worship;* the celebration of God's presence by God's people. We believe worship is relational. Worship is serving God with praise and allowing him to meet us at the point of our need. Worship allows us to experience God on a personal level, which in turn teaches us the importance of intimacy with one another. We teach our people about the importance of worship. We remind folks that just being in a room with other Christians on Sunday morning does not make them worshipers of God. Rather, to the degree that a person encounters God at some personal level is the degree to which that person is engaged in worship.

Worship is not performance. It is not people on a platform performing for people in a pew. Neither is worship people on a platform prompting people in a pew so that corporate performance is offered to an observing God. Worship is relational intimacy with God.

Community is developed and sustained through *shared lives.* We seek to share our lives together in a spirit of love, acceptance, unity, and forgiveness. Small groups, Sunday school classes, fellowship circles, etc., are essential components to relationship building at Union Chapel. We have many dozens of small groups that address a wide range of needs in our community of faith. We make small groups a priority because authentic relationships are God's design for us and because we want to resist our culture which breeds independence, isolation, and loneliness.

Community is fortified by the *preaching, teaching,* and *ongoing study of the Holy Scriptures.* When the understanding of the Word of God increases, the number of disciples will inevitably multiply. Maturing Christians continually submit to the teaching of the Scriptures. We honor the Scriptures at Union Chapel by teaching them in our small groups, Sunday school classes, and during midweek service.

Community is empowered through *prayer.* Prayer is the vehicle through which the church breathes. Prayer is the personal and corporate expression of communion, fellowship, and intimacy with God. Prayer is the power of the church, moving the heart and hand of God. John Wesley said, "God does nothing but in answer to prayer." We concur. Union Chapel has an intentional ministry of prayer through a 24-hour-a-day prayer room, supporting city-wide prayer summits, prayer vigils, calls for fasting and prayer, prayer walking, etc. Our staff meets for one hour of prayer together each week in addition to our program meetings.

Church in Mission

Second, we must be the church in *mission.* Out of the supportive, nurturing community flow the dynamics of authentic ministry. We must recognize our place in the body of Christ and then embrace an uncompromising commitment to carry out the mission of Jesus Christ (Matthew 28:19–20; Acts 1:8). We encourage everyone in our congregation to discover his and her particular gifts and then to exercise them on a regular basis.

We are currently focused on three segments of our community: the middle class, the inner-city poor, and the students of our local state university. We have discovered "servant evangelism" to be an effective tool in reaching the middle class. Servant evangelism involves doing simple acts of kindness (washing cars, mowing lawns, serving cold drinks at community events, etc.) that demonstrate the love of God in practical ways. For example, during the past two Christmas seasons we have offered free gift wrapping at the local shopping mall. Our teams wrapped more than 20,000 gifts. Our efforts among the inner-city poor include weekly food distribution, counseling services, tutoring, after-school latch key program, and, in association with another congregation, Sunday morning worship services in a store-front facility. The students of the university find our upbeat, contemporary music and worship style to be appealing. We also provide other on-campus activities for students.

Our ultimate vision is to plant churches "of the poor" in the inner cities of America and the world. Our current focus in on central Asia where we have sent out, from our local congregation, eight adults (plus their children) to plant churches. They are living in Asia, making friends, sharing Jesus, training the converts, raising up indigenous leaders, and planting churches among the unreached.

We believe that it is through mission that people find purpose in life, a focus for living, and real significance. Ministry and outreach become the expression of our intimacy with God and with one another. One of the reasons local churches stagnate spiritually is because they fail to comprehend the essential need for outreach. All living things need intake and outgo. The church is no different. Every local cluster of believers needs a clear understanding of their purpose and an intentional strategy to see that vision fulfilled. Purpose and vision flow out of prayer, a knowledge of your church's personality and gifts, and the felt needs of your community. At Union Chapel we continually ask three questions:

1. "What are our strengths as a staff and as a congregation?"
2. "What are the needs of the community?"
3. "What is God saying to us about those needs?"

As a practical way of discerning God's vision for your church, I would suggest you simply step outside the front door of your building and begin walking in increasing circles around the neighborhood. While you walk ask God for a vision, a sense of purpose. Pray that God will begin to touch your heart with the things that touch his heart. You will begin to see your world differently as God's vision possesses you. Without a dream there is drudgery and burnout. Without a vision people lose hope and give up (Proverbs 29:18). However, with a clearly stated purpose and a desire to work together in love and unity, great things, even miraculous things, can be accomplished for the glory of God.

Conclusion

Remember, the unchurched people of our culture no longer view the local church as the place where they should go to find answers. In today's world we must love people by reaching out to them in practical ways at the point of their need and offer the life-changing reality of Jesus Christ. The church must go and serve beyond the four walls of our buildings. People are desperately looking for answers. As one false god after another is found to be bankrupt, the truth of the gospel of Jesus Christ will become more appealing to people. The church of Jesus Christ is being handed a divine opportunity to change the course of redemptive history. It will require a church in community (people loving one another in authentic relationships) and a church in mission (people loving the lost and reaching out to them at the point of their need).

Floyd Zigler was already in his nineties when he introduced himself to me after I preached my first sermon at Union Chapel. He was the oldest living member of the church and actually assisted his father in the construction of the original church building. Floyd was a precious man of God whose witness was evident to everyone who knew him. Within months, Floyd's family moved him to a nearby city to live his last days in a retirement home. I visited Floyd on occasion and always came away enriched by his confident faith and compelling witness.

My last visit with Floyd was unique. During that visit we both sensed it would be our last meeting this side of heaven. We talked about a number of things pertaining to the faith and the great works of God. At the end of the visit I prayed for both of us. I hugged Floyd, stood to my feet, and took one step when he reached out and seized my hand. He pulled me down close to his face and as tears began to flow he said passionately, "When I joined the Methodist church in 1916, it was my ticket to glory!"

No other words were shared. They did not need to be. Within a few weeks Floyd was in the glorious presence of Jesus. His words continue to challenge and motivate me. May God grant to us sufficient grace so that the church in our generation is so vital and so authentic that the people who join our ranks will know that amazing grace of God and be made fit for eternal glory!

Questions

1. Why does the Church exist?
2. Do we need to go to church to be Christians?
3. Why do people go to church? Why do you go?
4. What made you choose your present church? Why do you continue to attend?
5. What aspects of church-life do you most appreciate?
6. What is the most memorable church service you have ever attended?
7. How would you explain the importance of the church to an unchurched friend?

Gregg Parris *A frequent speaker at conferences, churches, retreats, and youth camps, Rev. Parris is pastor of Union Chapel United Methodist Church in Muncie, Indiana which has grown in average worship attendance from 70 to more than 1,200 in the last 13 years. He received his M.Div from Asbury Theological Seminary and was recently awarded the W. J. Briggs Personal Evangelism Award from the North Indiana Conference. He is a member of the Advisory Board of the United Methodist Renewal Services Fellowship and the Board of Directors of the Mission Society for United Methodists. He and his wife Mary Beth have been married 20 years and have two sons.*

Chapter 13

Mission

by Dick McClain

Mission is a hot word today. No corporation worth the paper on which its annual report is printed can survive, much less thrive, without a "mission statement." Individuals are challenged to adopt a personal "mission statement" as the defining guide for their lives. Whether the aim is selling soft drinks or stocks, striving for physical mastery or personal serenity, individuals and groups alike don't want to be caught dead these days without a well-defined mission statement. Emil Brunner once stated, "As fire exists by burning, so the church exists by mission." In today's environment of mission mania, who could disagree?

Nevertheless the question remains, what is mission? Or more specifically, what is the church's mission? Before attempting to answer the question, it would be well to consider who can decide what the mission of the church is. If for example, the mission of the church can be selected from a smorgasbord of options by a group of people gathered for an annual planning retreat, then the mission could be almost anything. Judging from the variety of programs and priorities represented among congregations today, one wonders whether the whims of various members have not been accepted as the authority on which rests the mission of the church.

But the church is of God. Its head is none other than Jesus Christ. And as a consequence, its mission is not ours to choose, but his to declare. And declare it he has! God has not left his people in the dark about their mission.

The Great Commission

Shortly before returning to heaven, the Lord Jesus declared to his disciples, "All authority in heaven and on earth has been given to me. Therefore go and make disciples of all nations, baptizing them in the name of the Father and of the Son and of the Holy Spirit, and teaching them to obey everything I have commanded you" (Matthew 28:18–20a).

Jesus has the authority to declare and to define the church's mission. According to his own words, the mission of the church is to "go and make disciples." He even defined the nations of the world as the target of the church's mission. Once his authority is acknowledged, the question of the church's mission is forever settled, for he has declared it.

It is noteworthy that this "Great Commission" from our Lord is consistent with the announcement concerning his own personal mission statement, which was "to seek and to save what was lost" (Luke 19:10). His call to go to all the nations with the aim of making disciples is also part of an unbroken thread of revelation concerning God's eternal purposes, which are manifested consistently and repeatedly throughout both the Old and the New Testaments. From the call of Abram, in which God declared his intention that "all people on earth" would ultimately share in the blessing that was to come through Abram and his offspring (Genesis 22:18); to Isaiah's declaration that, since it would be "too small a thing" for the Servant of the Lord to restore only Jacob and Israel, God would make him a "light for the Gentiles" (Isaiah 49:6); to John's vision of the "great multitude that no one could count, from every nation, tribe, people and language, standing before the throne and in front of the Lamb" (Revelation 7:9). God's purpose has always been that people of every nation would be restored to fellowship with him. And since that is God's eternal purpose, it also defines his marching orders for the church, for the church's mission cannot differ from his.

Two Key Truths

Elsewhere in this book, two key truths that help us to understand the church's mission have been dealt with: the need of lost humanity and the redemption offered only through Jesus Christ. Because of the universal separation of humankind from God due to sin, all people everywhere stand equally in need of God's redemption, which was purchased with Jesus' own blood. That redemption is to be found nowhere else, precisely because it is the gift of God and not the achievement of humanity (Ephesians 2:8–9). As Peter declared before the Sanhedrin, "Salvation is found in no one else, for there is no other name under heaven given to men by which we must be saved" (Acts 4:12).

When the essential foundations of the Christian faith are crumbling, the eternal mission of the church is clouded. And when the mission focus is clouded, it is only a matter of time before zeal for "missions" is crippled. It is therefore not surprising that in a day when the twin truths of Jesus' atonement and humanity's lostness are increasingly challenged, at least in the old-line denominations, the church's mission of calling all people everywhere to discipleship has also come under attack. And when the church has denied its God-ordained mission, is it any wonder that programs of missions and evangelism have experienced radical decline? For example, between 1962 and

1979 there was a 46 percent drop in the number of missionaries
sent out by The United Methodist Church; a 68 percent decline
in the United Church of Christ; and a whopping 79 percent re-
duction in the Episcopal Church. One can hardly imagine a more
striking illustration of a lost sense of mission than this tragic
abandonment of once-vibrant programs of world missions and
evangelism among the old-line churches. And of course, the
decrease in missions abroad has been paralleled by a decline in
membership at home.

The early Methodists passionately embraced the church's
mission of winning the lost to Jesus Christ. First in England
and then in America, the Wesleyan movement was character-
ized by evangelistic zeal. It wasn't long before compassion for
the lost led Methodists to look to the unevangelized regions of
the world. When the Reverend Melville Cox, American
Methodism's first foreign missionary, was about to leave for
Liberia in the early 1830s, a friend scoffed at what he believed
was Cox's foolhardy plan. "If you go to Africa, you'll die there!"
he warned. "If I die, then you write my epitaph," was Melville's
quick retort. Caught off guard, his friend responded, "But what
should I write?" Cox's thoughtful answer is inscribed today on
a monument in his honor in Monrovia, Liberia: "Though a thousand fall, let not Africa be lost."

As the Apostle Paul expressed it, "Christ's love compels us"
(2 Corinthians 5:14). We cannot love him and not love the world
for which he died. We should devote our lives and our all to
making him known to all the world!

The Unfinished Task

Faithfulness to the church's mission today demands that we
analyze the unfinished task around the world and plan our response with strategic precision, identifying and reaching out to
those unreached people groups who have not yet had a chance to
hear or respond to the good news. Mission strategists tell us that

more than ten thousand such people groups do not yet have an indigenous church (defined by language, culture, and geography) of sufficient size and strength to be able, without outside assistance, to evangelize the remainder of their group. Mission efforts today must be planned with an eye to penetrating those unreached people groups. At the same time, we must redouble our evangelistic efforts among those massive population groups who may have heard the gospel but still have not heeded God's call to salvation in Jesus Christ. In other words, we need to be concerned about both the unreached and the unsaved!

The mission given to us by Jesus belongs to and is incumbent upon the church universal. Thankfully, the day has passed when cross-cultural missions are the sole domain of the Western churches. In fact, at a time when many Western denominations are curtailing programs of world missions, vibrant churches in the two-thirds world are launching new mission agencies by the hundreds and sending forth their own missionaries by the thousands. Some are even coming to America to evangelize us.

Just as missions today have a more international face than in previous generations, so the magnitude of human needs demands that our mission efforts in this generation be more holistic than ever before. By example and teaching Jesus declared his compassion for the whole person. He had no interest in merely saving souls while neglecting suffering bodies, consigning them to continue in their present misery. Even so, the church's mission programs must creatively and concretely address the alarming manifestations of such issues as poverty, hunger, suffering, and racism that hover like a death angel over the masses of people today.

Conclusion

The countdown to A.D. 2000 echoes louder with each passing day. Many "Great Commission Christians" have adopted the goal of finishing the unfinished task of taking the gospel to every people group by the end of this second Christian millennium. The task can be completed. Our mission can be fulfilled. One day it will be! If all God's people made Jesus' last command their first concern, there could really be a viable Christian witness among every group, tongue, and nation by the turn of the century, or at the very least by the end of this present generation. Jesus didn't give us an impossible mission; just one that requires that we move forward on our knees and in total dependence upon his Spirit. Whether ours will be the generation of which it can be said, "mission accomplished," remains to be seen. But my hope is that God will grant us the grace, the passion, and the vision to be faithful to his mission to reach all the world for Christ.

Questions

1. What is the mission of the Church? Is it important for the Church to have a mission? Explain.
2. How have you helped fulfill the mission of the Church?
3. Does your local church have a mission statement? If yes— What does it say?
4. How should the Church support missionaries? How are you involved?
5. Have you ever been on a mission trip? Have you ever served as a missionary?
6. What are some mission type successes you have seen or been a part of?
7. Can you suggest any ways that your church could do better in this area?

Dick McClain *Born in China of missionary parents, Rev. McClain grew up in India and Hong Kong. From 1971–1973 he participated in youth ministry in the Panama Canal Zone. Today his mission field experience serves him well in his position as Vice President for Mission Ministries for The Mission Society for United Methodists. Prior to joining The Mission Society, he was a pastor in the West Michigan Conference from 1975–1986. He received his M.Div. from Asbury Theological Seminary. He has been married to his wife Pam for 27 years. They live in Stone Mountain, Georgia and have three children.*

Chapter 14

Discipleship

by Robert E. Coleman

The command to reach the world for Christ resounds through the Gospels. Jesus commands his followers to go and disciple all people everywhere, baptizing believers and teaching them to do his will.

Traditionally we have interpreted this to mean a call to overseas missionary service. Certainly this is a priority concern. More people are needed in the mission fields of the world, especially in crossing cultural boundaries with the gospel. The number of men and women moving into this challenging ministry could well increase a hundredfold.

But is going to a distant land to work for Christ the only way to fulfill the command? A closer look at the commission in the Gospel of Matthew answers the question. "Go," "baptize," and "teach" all derive their force from "make disciples" (Matthew 28:19–20). The command is not to see how far one can travel in ministry, though the word "go" does stand in a coordinate relationship to the verb, emphasizing the necessity for taking the initiative in contacting people. Similarly, we baptize and teach in the process of reaching the world. But it is discipling that gives validity to the other activity.

The word "disciple" translates "learner." So a disciple of Christ is one who learns of him. Assuredly as one grows in the knowledge and grace of our Lord, there will be development in character, as well as maturation in ministry. Disciples inevitably become disciplers, reproducing again the cycle of growth.

A Closer Look at Jesus

To understand what this means we must look at Jesus and observe his way of life. As we do, we are made aware of a completely different value system. Renouncing his own rights in order to identify with our needs, he took the form of a servant, bearing our sorrows, carrying our grief and, finally, dying for our sin. As Jesus hung on the cross, people mocked him, saying, "He came to save others, but look at him! He can't even save himself!" (Matthew 27:42). The irony is that in their derision the crowd said the truth. Of course Jesus could not save himself. That was the point. He had not come to save himself. He came to save us. He came to seek and to save the lost. He came not to be served but to serve, and to give his life as a ransom for the world (Matthew 20:28).

On his pilgrimage to Calvary Jesus went about doing good, responding with compassion to the cry of the multitudes. Most people were appreciative, but blinded by materialism and self-centeredness; they had a superficial understanding of his message. Unless spiritual leadership could be raised up to multiply the ministry of Christ, there was no way the waiting harvest could be realized.

So while manifesting God's love and power to the people, Jesus cultivated those who someday would lead them. They were called to follow him. As their number grew, he chose 12 to be with him. Peter, James, and John had an even closer relationship, underscoring the principle that the smaller the group being taught, the greater the opportunity for learning.

Seldom were these men separated from him. For the better part of three years they lived and worked side by side. It was like a family, learning and growing together. In this close association the disciples were able to see the demonstration of Christ's teaching and to feel his burden for the people. Before long they were sent out to do much the same things Jesus had been doing: preaching, teaching, healing and, above all, making disciples. Though progress was painfully slow, especially in comprehending the meaning of the cross, Jesus patiently kept them moving toward his goal.

That vision was the ultimate evangelization of the world and the establishment of his eternal kingdom. By following his plan of discipling and appropriating the power of the Holy Spirit, his objective would be fulfilled.

The Role of Discipler

Our Lord has given us a model that every believer can follow. Too easily we have relegated his ministry to those persons who fit rather well-defined stereotypes of church work, such as the Sunday school teacher or preacher. Sometimes it is even more narrowly limited to trained personnel who are properly ordained or commissioned for service. However, most people cannot identify with these professional roles of ministry. For them the priesthood of all believers remains an elusive ideal. They may regard themselves as priests before God on the vertical level of prayer, but there is little, if any, comprehension of their priesthood on the horizontal plane of human relationships. This is because ministry has been equated with official church vocational callings, and not with the more undergirding servant role of discipler.

The Great Commission comes as a corrective to this popular misconception. In its focus upon lifestyle, our Lord's basic ministry becomes a meaningful option to every child of God. The homemaker, the farmer, and the automobile mechanic in their natural spheres of influence have as much occasion to follow Christ's example as does the evangelist or missionary. Some persons will have special roles for which they are gifted, and their discipling will take place through that calling, whether at home or abroad. But the Great Commission itself is not a special gift or calling; it is an intentional daily servant pattern of living by which learners are led in the way of Christ.

The responsibility to evangelize the world rests upon every Christian. No one can be excused on the basis of not being called. For Jesus has made it clear that his discipling ministry is woven into the fabric of Christian life, and its ultimate objective, through the power of the Holy Spirit, is to bring God's Good News to every person.

Practical Guidelines

The following deductions from Christ's example may suggest some practical guidelines:

1. Pray that the Lord will raise up laborers for his harvest—persons with the Shepherd's heart, who will learn his way and be willing to lay down their lives for the sheep.
2. Take the servant's mantle. It finds expression in the compassionate response we make to the needs of people, whether physical, social, or spiritual.
3. Be alert to those eager to learn of Christ. This yearning has been placed in the heart by God. A few such budding disciples are within the sphere of everyone's influence, beginning at home, and the environs where we live and work.
4. Get together with learners as much as possible. The more natural the association the better, like having dinner or playing ball together. Arrange some times for extended fellowship.
5. Accept a basic discipline to encourage obedience. That which is agreed on will depend upon the situation. It might be daily devotions, Bible study, Scripture memory, fasting or another form of abstinence, church work, personal witnessing or social action. Whatever it is, keep it relevant and growing.
6. Show how to minister. The emphasis is upon demonstration.

People will catch onto our schedule of priorities, burdens of prayer, and practice of witness in the context of living.

7. Involve each person in service according to his or her gifts. It is on-the-job training all the way. There is something everyone can do. As faith and skills grow, participation can be enlarged.

8. Keep them on course through continual supervision. Teach faithfulness in completing assignments. Always build self-esteem by personal affirmation and commendation.

9. Expect disciples to reproduce your vision for the kingdom. As the process repeats itself in other disciples, and they in turn do the same, your witness will continue to reach out in an ever-expanding sphere to the ends of the earth and to the end of time.

10. Let the Holy Spirit have his way. Here finally is the secret of the Great Commission. God's work can never be done in the energy of the flesh. As this is learned, the life of Jesus becomes real; he lives and works through his disciples, and we experience the overwhelming reality of the promise: "Lo, I am with you always, to the close of the age" (Matthew 28:20).

Questions

1. What is discipleship?
2. How did Jesus disciple people? Why did he do it?
3. Can you think of other Biblical characters who discipled other people?
4. What does the Great Commission (Matthew 28:18-20) mean?
5. Who should be involved in making disciples? Is it only for pastors and missionaries? Why or why not?
6. How do we make disciples today?
7. Have you ever been discipled? If so, how and by whom?

This article first appeared in *Decision* magazine in February 1986. Dr. Coleman has granted us permission to include it in its present form as part of this book on essential truths. All Scripture quotations are from the Revised Standard Version.

Robert E. Coleman   *Dr. Coleman is Director of the School of World Mission and Evangelism and Professor of Evangelism at Trinity International University. He also serves as Director of the Billy Graham Institute at Wheaton and Dean of the International Schools of Evangelism. He is a graduate of Asbury Theological Seminary, Princeton Theological Seminary, and received the Ph.D. from the University of Iowa. Dr. Coleman is a founding member of the Lausanne Committee for World Evangelization and president of Christian Outreach Foundation, and has been president of the Academy for Evangelism in Theological Education. He has written 21 books, including* The Master Plan of Evangelism, The Great Commission Lifestyle, *and* The Coming World Revival. *Dr. Coleman and his wife, Marietta, live in Deerfield, Illinois. They have three grown children.*

Chapter 15

Evangelism—
How to Know God

by Robert G. Tuttle, Jr.

Some months ago I was sitting in a sauna with a young man I did not know. As we were getting acquainted I soon found that he was a Muslim from Sri Lanka. At one point, I asked him if he had ever considered Christianity. He replied, "No, why should I?"

I responded, "What do you do for a living?" He was an engineer so I asked, "What do you do when you have a 50-ton block of concrete? How do you move it?"

He smiled a bit, "You've got to have a hoist."

My immediate response, "Let me tell you about the hoist." Quickly I explained about the power of the Holy Spirit available through faith in Jesus Christ. As I left the sauna I motioned with my hand pretending to raise an imaginary block, "Remember the hoist." Somewhat to my surprise he smiled again and promised he would not forget. The next day I caught sight of him across a crowded room. When he saw me he motioned by raising his hand, pretending to lift an imaginary object.

Every religion the world over is like a 50-ton block of concrete. It is impossible to move without a hoist. That hoist is the power of the Holy Spirit available through faith in Jesus Christ. That illustrates the difference between religion (a 50-ton block of "do's and don'ts") and a personal relationship with God through faith in Jesus Christ (the power of the gospel).

Recently on an airplane I was visiting with a Roman Catholic. He stated that "Catholics tend to identify being a Christian with membership in the church as an organization, but the church means nothing to me. I'm one unhappy puppy." Then he asked, "What do Protestants believe?" I said quite simply that although church membership is important to most Protestants, we tend to identify being a Christian with a personal relationship with Jesus Christ. He seemed interested. We talked for more than two hours about the difference between Christianity as a religion and Christianity as a relationship.

Several years ago I was given the responsibility of taking the theology of the Roman Catholic Cursillo and making it more consistent with Protestant Christianity—the Emmaus Walk. Immediately I realized that I needed to turn the theology of the Cursillo on its head. Roman Catholic theology (taking its lead from Thomas Aquinas) assumes that religion has to do more with doing—performance. Protestants (taking their lead from reformers like Luther, Calvin, and Wesley) assume that Christianity is related first to being—relationship.

Christianity as Religion—Against Self-Reliance

Having a form of godliness without the power has been problematic for Christians since Pentecost, almost 2,000 years ago. According to the Apostle Paul (Romans 8:1–2), religion, in and of itself, is a law of sin and death. It is the law without the power or the inclination to obey it. Little wonder the Bible insists that one of the biggest sins is self-reliance. The truth is we cannot fulfill the law on our own steam. We must have help. Although one day we will be judged according to our works, obedience must be empowered by the Holy Spirit, who is available through faith in Jesus Christ. Let me tell you more about him.

No one finds God as if he were a thing discoverable by toil and instinct. God is known for one reason. He has revealed himself supremely in Jesus Christ and he has spoken the truth of that revelation clearly through a book—the Bible. John Wesley writes in the preface to his "Forty-four Sermons":

> Oh, give me that book! At any price, give me the book of God! I have it: here is knowledge enough for me. Let me be "*homo unius libri*" [a man of one book]. Here am I, far from the busy ways of men. I sit down alone: only God is here. In his presence I open, I read his book; for this end, to find the way to heaven.*

The Bible is our primary source for knowing God. All things necessary for salvation are therein contained. "The word of God is living and active. Sharper than any double-edged sword, it penetrates even to dividing soul and spirit, joints and marrow; it judges the thoughts and attitudes of the heart" (Hebrews 4:12). The Bible establishes doctrine and moral teaching. It speaks clearly and to the point. There is no fine print. God reveals; God does not conceal. So the Word alone is the starting place. To start anywhere else is to betray our method.

Christianity as Relationship

Jesus told us that we are grafted into the branch that is his body, through personal faith in him as Lord and Savior (John 15:1-8). To know God is to establish a relationship with him by placing our faith and trust in his provision for our salvation. Allow me to illustrate this point.

Recently I was in Cuba. One of our young communist guides took us to a square in old Havana. As we were standing before a rather imposing statue, I asked: "Who is that?"

---

*John Wesley, "Forty-four Sermons" (The Epworth Press, 1944), p. vi.

With obvious pride the guide said, "That is one of our greatest patriots, Carlos Manuel de Cespedes."

I asked, "What did he do?"

He said, "He was the first to free his slaves in 1865 and the
first to organize a resistance movement against the Spanish oppressor."

I was impressed, "That is wonderful."

The guide said, "Yes, but there is more. The Spaniards cap-
tured his son and threatened to kill him if he did not back down
from the resistance. When he refused, they murdered his son."

I winced, "That's horrible."

His enthusiasm seemed to build, "Yes, but there is more. Our
forefathers so identified with his example that the relationship
between this great patriot and the Cuban people led to our independence and Cuba became a Republic in 1902."

I had an insight, "There is an interesting precedent for all of
that. God established a covenant with a people, and when they
were enslaved he freed them from the Egyptian oppressor."

The guide said, "That is wonderful."

I said, "Yes, but there is more. God also chose to free the
people from the power of sin and offer forgiveness to those who
place their faith in his Son Jesus Christ."

The guide said, "Yes, I've heard. Is it important?"

I said, "Yes, but there is more. Our freedom cost God the life
of his only Son as an atonement for sin."

The guide said, "That's too bad."

I said, "Yes, but there is more. God raised his Son from the
dead and has sent us his Spirit that we might be victorious over
sin and death."

The guide asked, "How does that work?"

I said, "Just as your forefathers identified with the example
of Carlos Manuel de Cespedes that you might be free from the
Spanish oppressor, God asks that we identify with him by placing our faith and trust in his Son, Jesus Christ. Would you be
willing to trust God as your forefathers trusted Carlos Manuel de

Cespedes, that you might be freed from the power of sin and death?"

He said, "I think I would."

Knowing God is not "Grunt and groan," it is "repent and believe."

Some years ago a pastor introduced me to the most spiritual man in his church. As I gave the invitation at the end of my sermon, the first ones to the communion rail were the most spiritual man in the church and his wife. As I knelt to pray with them she whispered that she was carrying a horrible secret and would I please pray for her. I did pray as best I could. As she returned to her pew, her husband leaned across the communion rail and whispered : "You've got to pray for me, I'm her secret. I'm an alcoholic and you've got to pray that I get will power." In an instant, I insisted: "Dear brother, you don't need will power. You need the Holy Spirit."

Under the law when we sin, repent, and sin again, we are incapable of believing in the kind of good God who would hear such feeble repentance. Christianity as a religion does that to us. Our sin only seems to compound after repeated failure. The effect is this—every time we renew our repentance and faith under grace we have a fresh start, a new beginning. The Holy Spirit renews and refreshes so that our next inclination to sin is to resist the temptation. True spirituality is not accessed by the law of sin and death—grunt and groan—no power and no inclination to obey it. True spirituality is accessed by the law of the Spirit of life—repent and believe—empowered by the Holy Spirit. Knowing God is to trust his son, receive his forgiveness, and walk in his Spirit.

Here is a prayer that I believe is a slam dunk for establishing or renewing a right relationship with God:

> "Dear God, as an act of repentance, as far as I know my
> own heart, I am willing for You to take from me any area
> of my life not yet yielded to You. I give You any area of
> resistance so that Your will for my life would be accom-

plished. At the point of that repentance, I want to place my faith and trust in You and in Jesus Christ, Your provision for my sins, that I might experience the power of Your Holy Spirit for a new life in You. Amen."

Now let God arise!

Questions

1. How do we get to know God? Can anyone come to God?
2. How can religion be like a 50-ton block of concrete? Have you ever felt that way?
3. Are there certain steps we should follow in coming to Christ?
4. What is repentance? Who needs to repent and why?
5. Why do people need the Lord?
6. Have you ever led someone to Christ?
7. How can you be a better witness for Christ?

Robert G. Tuttle, Jr. *Today a professor at Asbury Theological Seminary, Dr. Tuttle has served as professor at Garrett-Evangelical Theological Seminary, Oral Roberts University, and Fuller Theological Seminary. He has also been a local pastor. He received the M.A. at Wheaton, B.D. at Garrett-Evangelical Theological Seminary, and Ph.D. at the University of Bristol in England. The author of many articles and books, including* Someone Out There Needs Me, Sanctity without Starch, *and* John Wesley: His Life and Theology. *Dr. Tuttle and his wife live in Brentwood, Tennessee and have five children.*

Chapter 16

Prayer

by Terry Teykl

When I was pastoring, I would occasionally go to the sanctuary early on Sunday mornings and walk through the rows of chairs, praying as I went. I could picture the faces of the people who would occupy those seats over the next few hours. Their hurts and needs would scroll through my mind: Ben lost his job last week; the Gordon's 15-year-old daughter is pregnant; Mike and Ellen are separated, heading for divorce; and Brenda's cancer is spreading, despite the fervent prayers of friends and intercessors. They would all come to church, desperately wanting to hear a word of hope, but I had only one message and 20 short minutes. How could I speak to each of them?

Praying for Vision

As a preacher, you cannot preach truth simply because it is interesting to you. You must seek a vision and direction for your people and hear from God what aspect of truth to proclaim at every opportunity. When you take time to be alone with God, searching and listening patiently for his voice, he will give you the vision—his vision. He cares about the hurts and needs of each person who sits in church on Sunday morning. If pastors take the time to seek him, he will give them words to minister to his people.

There is a vast difference between just "getting a sermon" and pressing into God until a particular truth grabs you and throws you down in a headlock. I remember at my own Annual Conference several years ago watching pastors raiding the book table looking for sermon material. Some were close to retirement; others just looked tired. I realized as I watched that without a fresh vision, we quickly become mechanical—researching the latest literature to find a sermon we have not yet preached, scraping together just enough material to get us through another Sunday morning. If there is no vision in the pulpit, there will be no vision in the pews.

To hear from God and stay spiritually "fueled up," pastors need time alone to pray. Ironically, pastors are sometimes so busy praying for others and trying to minister to the needs of their flock that they have little time to be alone with God. Every phone call seems critical; every meeting seems important. Many are trapped by the tyranny of rushing from crisis to crisis, only to find themselves in the pulpit on Sunday morning physically exhausted and spiritually drained. I know that feeling all too well.

But consider Jesus. In Mark 1:35, we read, "Very early in the morning, while it was still dark, Jesus got up, left the house and went off to a solitary place, where he prayed, . . . and when [the disciples] found him, they exclaimed: 'Everyone is looking for you!'" Luke records, ". . . the news about him spread all the more, so that crowds of people came to hear him and to be healed of their sicknesses. But Jesus often withdrew to lonely places and prayed" (Luke 5:1 5–16). Jesus knew he was in demand. The people searched for him. Many were sick and some were dying. They needed miracles and healing. Many wanted only to be near Jesus, to touch his garments, and listen to his teaching. Yet Jesus was not rushing from place to place, as the disciples probably thought he should. He took time to be alone with his Father, and the people had to wait because Jesus understood the urgency of prayer. It was the lifeline of his ministry.

If you are a pastor, examine your schedule. Are you taking time to wait on God, allowing him to give you fresh vision for your congregation? Or are you spiritually bankrupt, flipping through pages of the latest book to find another last-minute message? Insist on time to pray. If you are a church leader or layperson, make sure that your pastor is encouraged, supported, and has time away. Here are some practical suggestions:

- Develop a team of lay ministers who can respond to needs and crises during the week. This is scriptural and will help prevent pastoral burnout.
- Build a team of intercessors to pray for church members by name every day.
- John Case, a pastor in Jackson, Mississippi, never takes calls or appointments before 11:00 a.m. He spends early mornings alone with God.
- John Maxwell, Jack Hayford, and several other pastors go to the sanctuary early each Sunday morning to pray for their message and for the people.
- When I was pastoring, I took every Thursday off to study and pray.
- Many pastors find it helpful to schedule two or three days each month to pray. Often they find it necessary to leave town or go to a secluded place.

Powerful Preaching

Several years ago, my wife and I traveled to Buenos Aires to see firsthand a great move of God. We had the opportunity to visit a church called "Waves of Love and Peace," pastored by a former street fighter and drug dealer, Hector Jimenez. The church literally had services around the clock, breaking only at midnight to clean the floors. Every service was packed! I preached the "early service" on Sunday morning—1:00 a.m.—and the sanctuary was three-fourths full, with people standing outside waiting to get in for the next one. It was absolutely amazing. The people were so hungry for a touch from God that they actually trampled my shoes when I stepped off the platform during my sermon.

After the service, I asked Hector a simple question: "Why?" He led me down a dark hallway behind the pulpit and stopped in front of a door. "Everything that goes on out there is a result of what is happening in here," he said. He pushed open the door, revealing 10 or 12 women, face down, fervently praying back the forces of darkness and inviting the Holy Spirit to come.

Prayer like that was not a new concept to me. In my own church in College Station, Texas, I had many who prayed for me during the week as well as on Sunday morning as I preached. I knew that no matter where I was, when I stood up to speak, others hit their knees to pray, and I was always comforted by that. But that experience in Buenos Aires was a clear reminder that any sermon I preach is only as powerful as the prayer force behind it. Three-point messages, poems, illustrations, examples, and even testimonies can inspire people to come to Christ, but only when the Holy Spirit uses these devices to convict sinners of their need to repent. Only the Holy Spirit can draw a person into the saving knowledge of Jesus. Preaching, if it is not anointed with prayer and delivered through the power of the Holy Spirit, is like throwing a fistful of dust into the wind. It may sting and irritate for a few brief moments, but it is easily brushed off and forgotten.

The Holy Spirit comes when people pray. In the book of Acts, we read that the disciples preached so powerfully that hundreds at a time were added to their number and many people were healed. But it is important to note that when they were not preaching, they were praying. They did not schedule prayer meetings, they lived them. In Luke 9, Jesus took Peter, James, and John up a mountain to pray; the Scripture says, "As [Jesus] was praying, the appearance of his face changed, and his clothes became as bright as a flash of lightning" (v. 29). Jesus was transfigured *as he was praying.*

As a pastor, you need intercessors who will lift you up as you preach, and who will pray for those receiving the message to be open to the Holy Spirit. As I have worked with pastors all over the county, I have seen several ways this can be done:

- Gather with a group of leaders early Sunday morning to pray for the message and for those who will hear it.

- If your church has a prayer room, record the title and Scripture for each week's sermon on a taped message so that intercessors can pray over it all week.

- Jimmy Buskirk, pastor of First United Methodist Church in Tulsa, Oklahoma, has a different group of men who pray for him during each service.

- Ask a youth Sunday school class to pray for the message before they begin their lesson.

- Announce from the pulpit any occasions when you will be speaking during the coming week, such as at weddings or funerals, and ask people to pray specifically during those times for the message, not just for the event or families.

Ministering through Prayer

If you have sought a vision for your people, and then bathed it in prayer, people will respond. When the Holy Spirit pierces souls with the truth of Jesus, their repentance or commitment needs to be sealed in prayer. You preach with the purpose of imparting truth and bringing the unsaved to the point of seeing their need for God, and you must go the next step by praying for those who respond. Prayer is the means we have of ministering to the needs that arise once the Gospel has been proclaimed.

Unfortunately, prayer at the altar is a lost art in too many churches. All too often I visit with people who say they have been attending church regularly for years, but have never been prayed for personally. How tragic that hurting humanity can come to church looking for comfort and compassion, and receive nothing but a bulletin and a three-point sermon! As pastors we must not be satisfied simply to find the truth ourselves, or even to communicate it passionately and eloquently to our flocks. We must do all we can to see to it that our people do not leave our services in the same condition in which they came.

The altar rails that stand in churches today were originally known as "the mourners' bench." On their knees, believers cried out to God for hours at a time, seeking personal forgiveness or praying for the lost to be saved. As time passed those benches evolved into communion rails, and then into fences meant to keep the pastor in and the people out. They lost their true meaning. The good news is that prayer as a ministry is now finding its way back into many mainline churches, rekindling the fervent prayer that took place at the mourners' benches of old.

Making prayer a priority in the service is just one expression of a literal prayer explosion that is happening across the earth today. Dr. Peter Wagner says that prayer is reaching "epidemic proportions," as the Holy Spirit has sparked awakening in churches and cities everywhere. Churches are training lay people to pray at the altar with those who have needs, and they are learning to continue to pray as long as it takes to find help. God does not shut down at noon; in fact he desires that we always be open to how he might use us to minister his love, whether we are at work, in the shopping mall, or even at church.

As you build your altar ministry, train workers so that they can pray effectively. As a pastor, I trained my lay ministers with the following guidelines:

■ Come to the altar at the leading of the pastor.

■ Let men pray with men, women with women.

- Listen for the seeker to tell you of needs so you will know how to pray. Don't be shocked by what you hear.

- Ask for permission to pray.

- Pray Scriptures over the person.

- Refer serious problems to the pastoral staff.

- Take distressed people into a private room to pray.

- Have boxes of tissue available.

- Practice team praying when possible. While one is speaking to the seeker, the other prays.

- Make pertinent materials available for those who receive prayer.

Mark Rutland is not only one of the best preachers in the country, he is also one of the most disciplined in his personal prayer life. He was preaching one Thanksgiving at Lee College, when he felt strongly impressed to abandon the sermon he had prayerfully prepared and to give his testimony. He told about a low point in his life and ministry when he was so discouraged that he put a gun into his mouth. In that pit of despair, God reached in and pulled him out, giving his life new meaning and turning his ministry around. After the message, a young man approached Mark and handed him a small gun that he had in his pocket. The student had wandered in that morning, depressed and suicidal, and was utterly amazed by what he heard. Because Mark was "prayed up," God was able to use him to save a young man's life. He keeps that small gun in a special place in his home as a reminder that proclamation must be preceded, accompanied, and followed by prayer. Souls and lives are at stake.

Questions

1. Why is prayer an important part of preaching? Does your church have altar calls?
2. What should we pray about?

3. Why does God tell us to pray? Has God limited his involvement by waiting for us to pray?
4. Is there anything we shouldn't pray for? Can you back up your answer from the Bible?
5. Do you have a daily time set aside to pray? Where do you like to pray?
6. How can you pray more strategically for your pastor and church leaders?
7. What are some answers to prayer that you specifically recall? Why is it important to remember those times?

Terry Teykl   Drawing on his 28 years of experience as a pastor, Rev. Teykl leads a ministry focusing on prayer and evangelism. Having begun a church with only eight people who were committed to prayer, Aldersgate United Methodist church grew to more than 1,000 members in five years. He produces prayer resources that teach people how to pray with purpose and understanding. He received his M.Div. from Perkins School of Theology and the Doctorate of Ministry from Oral Roberts University. He has written many books, articles, and study guides, including Preyed On or Preyed For, Making Room to Pray, *and* Acts 29. *He and Kay, his wife of 38 years, live in Spring, Texas. They have four grown children.*

Chapter 17

Church Growth

by Rose Sims

If you can dream it, you can do it! From a fledgling sect after its organization in 1784, Methodism grew from a few thousand to the largest denomination in the land. It surpassed the Baptists by 20 percent, and had as many members as Episcopalians, Congregationalists, and Presbyterians combined. By 1850, more than one-fourth of all professing Christians in America were Methodist. Had that rate of increase continued for a few more generations, every man, woman and child on the continent would have been won to Christ and been called a Methodist. How did they do it? Wesley gave us the five point, foolproof, guaranteed, unfailing ingredients for church growth:

1. You have nothing to do but save souls.
2. You have nothing to do but be a missionary church.
3. You have nothing to do but believe the Bible.
4. You have nothing to do but live a holy life.
5. You have nothing to do but make disciples of all men. (Then you have nothing left to do but rejoice.)

This is not a "how to" chapter on church growth. It is a simple narrative of that foolproof strategy at work. For the past 40 years I have put those principles to work in ordinary churches, often in seemingly impossible situations. With great joy I have watched those dead and dying churches go from despair to hope, often leading the state in professions of faith. We never deviated from Wesley's plan. I wonder why we try to fix Wesley's strategy when it still works perfectly. It is not a mere theory. It works. Here is the proof.

Oscar

On the fatal day when Hitler invaded Norway, a young Viking visionary, with ticket and seminary scholarship in hand and a dream in his heart, watched the old sea captain hoisting the final gangplank on the last boat leaving Norway. Hitler came to Norway to replace the Cross with the hated Swastika and the Bible with *Mein Kampf.* Hitler was a man who knew his history. Where once Luther had nailed his Ninety-five Theses and Zwingli, Hubmaier, and Wesley had dared defy Satan, churches stood empty. Having rejected the Bible as the authority, the Cross as the way of salvation, and Wesley's edict to "Offer them Christ" as outmoded, the churches had nothing to offer. Hitler's firm conviction was that all it takes to become a godless world is to create one generation of children and youth who know nothing about God and one generation of adults who don't care. When the church in Europe was most needed, it was empty, voiceless, and impotent.

Oscar had searched the harbor daily for cabin space and had the opportunity to share his dream with the saintly old harbormaster. Every cabin was packed to capacity, every inch of deck claimed by the hundreds of Jewish refugees fleeing the Holocaust. The harbormaster was now hoisting the gangplank! A tug at the sleeve, a prophetic order defying all protocol: "Get on board. Take your dream to America. Prove with your life that as the church goes, so goes the nation." So began Oscar's adventure.

The ship's log in Ellis Island for that day had one clean extra page with just one name, Oscar Grindheim.

My Life

I had been led to Christ by a dynamic rural pastor who was radically saved and whose burden for souls was contagious. His battle cry was "Whatever you do, don't go to heaven alone." I have never met a greater soul winner, nor have I ever been able to escape the vision that one day heaven will be every person's most imperative need.

It was in my third year at seminary that I first met this young, brilliant, and popular Viking, Oscar. Everywhere I turned, I met people he had quietly led to Christ. It was in a class in which Nietzsche's "God is dead" theory and the decline of the church in America had been discussed that Oscar quietly shared his dream. "I came to America when America was number one in the world in faith, church attendance, medicine, technology, education, morals, and family values. If the church loses its purpose, if evangelism is mere talk without fruit, is it possible that one day America could be number one in crime, divorce, drugs, alcoholism, illegitimacy and a greater mission field than Africa? He who does not learn from history is bound to repeat it." In that moment, I knew we were kindred spirits. We were married in August.

Our First Appointment

Dream in hand, we crossed the windy, barren Nebraska prairie to our first student pastorate. I saw a nearly closed ramshackle one-room country church. Oscar saw a rebuilt church packed with the least, the lost, and the lonely. It was a dream I was never able to escape during the twenty-seven years we ministered together. It was his legacy to me when God called him home. Soul winning is an art that has to be lived to be understood.

The sun was setting in blazing splendor and the steeple was casting its shadow across the weed-grown cemetery. "Let's slip off our shoes." Hand in hand, we circled the church, claiming every inch as holy ground. As the sun sank, we knelt and I heard Oscar claim every lost soul in that town for Jesus and pledge to give his all to make it happen.

The next day was Sunday. At 11:00 the church was empty. Faith never wavering, Oscar suggested, "Play the piano. We will sing." Then I heard his unfaltering rich bass voice singing in affirmation.

My hope is built on nothing less
Than Jesus' blood and righteousness.
I dare not trust the sweetest frame,
But wholly lean on Jesus' Name!

The invocation was a praise of thanks for all those who would be won to Christ. The worship proceeded as if the church were full. Oscar and I continued singing, "Only believe! Only believe! All things are possible! Only Believe!" By the fourth verse, we were joined by 14 latecomers. The previous student pastor never arrived until 11:20. Why bother? The church was closing. The Bible says, "Where there is no vision, the people perish" (Proverbs 29:18). In glory no music will ever sound sweeter than the robust singing of those salt-of-the-earth country saints.

During the rest of that hour something happened that can be attributed only to the Holy Spirit and faith. Clearly something was happening that was not in the bulletin. Oscar quietly spoke of the reality of his dream for America and this church with such love, passion, simplicity, and urgency that when he gave the first altar call in many years, all 14 persons responded. Kneeling at the altar with tears, they dedicated themselves to make the vision a reality. They rose from their knees with a priceless new commodity called *hope*. Then I heard Oscar's familiar benediction, which I would hear week after week, "If you can dream it, you can do it. The worship is over and the service has begun."

Leadership is always action, not position. After the potluck, those ordinary saints in overalls learned that goals must be biblical, specific, measurable, achievable, realistic, smart, and timely. Together around those homemade tables they asked the questions that led them to affirm Wesley's strategy and to write their first purpose statement: "The purpose of our church is to seek and save the lost and make disciples."

On Monday afternoon, the women of the church came bringing chickens and eggs and offerings from their gardens. The excuse was to help us get settled in our tiny four-room parsonage, but the real reason was to ask, "What do we do now?" A dream without action is like gold resting in the darkness of the mine. I sensed they were miles ahead of me, expecting after yesterday that God would somehow send another miracle today. Why not? Miracles come in many ways. Our miracle came at 3:30 promptly when the elementary school at the top of the hill dismissed a boisterous herd of school kids with nothing to do until supper. They came thundering right past the front door of the church. I didn't hear the miracle. I was busy making coffee for the ladies. They heard it. They were busy listening for a miracle. Children had stormed by the church door for years. They had always been somebody else's responsibility. Until now! "That's it!" said one mother. "My kids are growing up knowing nothing about God. Why don't we start an after school Kid's Klub?"

Nothing is so powerful as an idea whose time has come. Dreams aren't taught. They are caught. Every congregation is a risk taker, a caretaker, or an undertaker. Those who say it can't be done are usually passed up by others doing it. A goal is a dream with a deadline. We knew that not everything could be changed, but then nothing can ever be changed until it is faced.

Growth is the only evidence that there is life in a church. I saw those few laypeople grow and stretch as they turned ideas into innovations. Jump-starting a country church is largely a matter of hanging on after others have let go. It is doing the undoable, trying the impossible, believing the unbelievable. That little church knew that if we always do what we've always done, we will always get what we always got. Growth is nothing more than trying new ideas, letting go of what doesn't work and keeping what does work. The defining element is hard work, God's Word, and prayer. We laughed, we sang, we made friends and we cemented fellowships that lasted a lifetime. We had to dig into God's Word and develop our prayer lives. A wonderful ethnic pastor once told me, "You can't no more give somebody something you ain't got than you can come back from some place you ain't been."

The church was growing. Latent talent was discovered and put to work. They hung banners outside, put posters in every merchant's window, and advertised in the newspaper and on the radio. They shared their dreams wherever they went. Word of mouth is always the cheapest and most effective advertisement.

Honest mistakes are evidence that somebody tried something. The only ones who never make a mistake are those who do nothing, and that is the biggest mistake of all. Problems are only opportunities awaiting solutions, a wake-up call for creativity. By the end of the week, those fired-up lay folks had decided they would have a clown, a kitchen band, games, music, and a prize for the child who made the best poster for the merchants' windows downtown. And, of course, at every activity they would present the way of salvation. The main thing is to keep the main thing the main thing. They learned to share the simple plan of salvation with the old-fashioned wordless book: one page black for sin, the next red for the blood of Jesus, then white for forgiveness, gold for heaven, and green for growth. For craft time every child would make a wordless book to share with his or her family. Too many people make soul winning too complicated. It is just one lame man telling another lame man how he was healed! A grandmother, nearly 90, who couldn't sing or teach, rounded up her grandkids and together they furnished warm chocolate chip cookies and ice cold milk. What a talent! What a tool for evangelism! What a way to start an intergenerational church!

There were 30 kids in that first Kid's Klub. Life sometimes hands you a magical moment. This was ours and we savored it. I love to go to a dying church because the sturdy few who have survived the naysayers are usually those to whom their church is a priceless treasure, well worth paying any price to revive. Churches do not die easily. A great fire needs only a tiny spark. Great people are ordinary people who commit themselves to extraordinary things. Those few had nursed the dying church and sat weeping at her death bed. Dissension had nearly closed the church, but they learned that there are no mistakes in life, only lessons. Oscar preached that one unkind word may forever turn a lost soul from the church. Kind words are easy to speak and their echoes are endless. Before you speak, ask yourself, "Is it kind? Is it true? Is it necessary?"

Wesley's strategy read: "Be a missionary church." As we called on those children's parents and in the community, we saw enormous physical, emotional, spiritual, economic, and relational needs. It was easy to see why walking through the church door on Sunday morning was low on their list of priorities. So why not open the windows first? The Kid's Klub was just the first of many windows. How were we to know that one day that club would encompass almost 200 children whose lives for eternity would be forever changed?

A Saturday recreation program was next. Then a clothing giveaway and exchange followed. "Share Your Garden" eventually led to a food program that established us as a mission outreach even across county lines. Through the years folks have tried small groups, Scouts, adult education, singles, counseling, tutoring, divorce recovery, country western gospel sings, dinners for eight, dinner theater, SHARE food program, drama for youth, latchkey, health clinics, sports programs, musicals, drama, Alcoholics Anonymous, NARC, spouse abuse, and scores of other open windows. What wonderful fellowships grew from those events. We taught our laity the art of hospitality and friendship. A stranger should be greeted within three minutes of coming to a meeting, possibly even in the parking lot. We have all been to a new church where we felt as if we were attending someone else's family reunion. Every day you have two choices, to be happy or to be sad. We made it a habit to be happy. Folks wanted to see Jesus in us, a happy Jesus with skin on.

We programmed to the purpose, budgeted to the purpose, trained to the purpose, and evaluated by the purpose. Of each program we asked, "Is it winning the lost and growing disciples, or are we only doing what some good atheist is probably already doing better?" It was *hard work* but as one of the local saints remarked, "If we want this church to grow, we shouldn't itch for anything we aren't willing to scratch for." It meant getting involved to the point of inconvenience.

The task of the pastor is to equip the laity for evangelism. This means intentionally training every convert not only how to win the lost, but to inspire, organize, and give leadership opportunities so that they can succeed. We knew that a church with a great spiritual vision can easily fail if the leader does not have a good work ethic. We have tried many good programs: the Roman Road, Evangelism Explosion, the ABCs, and the wordless book. They are all good, but few churches rise above their leadership. However, when lay people were trained, they actually took over a lion's share of the load. In our first church, we encouraged them to get intentionally involved socially with the unchurched, invite them to dinner, take them to a ball game, be a friend with the specific intention of one day sharing Christ with them.

Wesley said, "Believe God's word and live a holy life." Bible study and prayer was spontaneous and became habitual because the purpose was clear. Those laypeople studied to keep ahead of their own children. They prayed because they knew they needed God's help. They visited because they had a burden for the families whose children were accepting the Lord. I don't think God cares how we worship, whether the style is liturgical or less formal; whether we sing the grand old hymns or the new inspiring praise and worship songs. Raising your hand in worship is most meaningful when you also raise your hand to volunteer to teach, or visit, or witness, or even to clean the church. It is what happens after the benediction and before the invocation that determines the quality of worship on Sunday morning.

Primary in our purpose was Wesley's admonition, "You have nothing to do but save souls and make disciples." So at the intermission of a dinner theater or bowling party, or some other outreach event, we had a layperson or the pastor take five minutes to say something like this:

"Aren't we having a good time at church tonight? Just as the school's purpose is education and the doctor's purpose is healing, so God gave the church the greatest purpose of all. It is to make sure that all know they will spend eternity in heaven. Would you mind if I asked you the most important question you will ever be asked? Have you come to the place in your spiritual life that you know for certain that you have eternal life? Jesus said, 'I am the way. He that believes on the Son of God has eternal life, and he that does not believe, shall not see life, but the wrath of God abides on him.' The little welcome card we gave you as you came in explains that being a Christian is as easy as ABC. A = ADMIT you are a sinner. B = BELIEVE on the Lord Jesus Christ. C = CHOOSE Christ and make him the Lord of your life. Does that make sense to you? Let me tell you briefly how I came to know for certain that I have eternal life. *(At this point the speaker shares very briefly a testimony of how Christ changed his or her life. Then everyone prays in unison the sinner's prayer printed on the card.)* If you accepted Christ for the first time when we prayed that prayer, we'd like to help you to understand the decision you just made by visiting with you. If you have other needs that our church could meet, check the appropriate box on the card. Feel free to add a comment if you have any ideas about ways our church family can help you better. If you would like to volunteer to help in any way, you are always welcome and needed. Just let us know how we can fellowship better."

Through the years we saw hundreds accept Christ at non-church events. Our attractive, informative, newsy, sometimes funny newsletter went out to hundreds. (We never sent out a sloppy, dull, poorly designed newsletter because it was the public's photo of who we were.) As prospects were followed through, many who accepted Christ later stood at the altar to make their profession public and to join the church. In fact, nearly 100 accepted Christ at the Country Western Gospel night in our last church. Many of those new converts became leaders in a calling program that encompassed the many who came through the doors or the windows of our church. Wesley said that most of us would like to believe that God is too loving to send a person to hell. What we fail to realize is that God cannot violate his own integrity. Though infinite in love, he is also holy and cannot ignore sin. Yet love is painful. Seeing our utter lostness, God took upon himself to die on the cross for a world of lost sinners.

Farewell

When the day came for us to move on we knew the church was ready for a full-time pastor. It had been hard work, but we had all learned so much about church growth. The last day, after the farewells had all been said and the folks had all gone home, Oscar and I stood for the last time on that holy ground. We took off our shoes and circled the church one last time. As we knelt in prayer, the full moon shone down on the rebuilt debt-free church, youth center, and social hall which had been packed to capacity that morning. Defining the purpose had built a praying, united, working laity, grounded in the faith and God's Word.

The years passed quickly as we went to other churches and saw the same kind of growth in every one of them. Were they all easy? No. Was God always faithful? Yes.

Oscar Goes Home

I was certain that our love for God and for each other was so strong that our family was unsinkable. I was sure it would last forever. But as Oscar winged his way gloriously to eternity his last words to me were, "Keep the dream alive! Make America see it can happen anywhere! Prove it with your life!"

The unbelievable pain of loss made me doubt the dream for the first time. I had five children to support: one in medical school, another at the conservatory of music, one in college and two nine-year-old adopted sons, plus a heavy load of teaching at the college. I wonder if stormy weather is what God sends from time to time to remind us we are never really in charge of anything.

We buried Oscar's broken body in a little pioneer cemetery adjacent to a closing Methodist church (Oscar's newest appointment) in the middle of an Amish cornfield. The next day, with my two sons beside me, we took off our shoes, and claimed every inch of the church's property as holy ground. Through eyes dimmed with tears, we dreamed about the new church and the souls that would be won.

Eight years later, when the new debt-free church was filled and ready for a full-time pastor, it was time for me to take a sabbatical. I had been accepted for post-doctoral research at Harvard. Bishop Goodrich asked me to help two more little dying country churches until I went east in the fall. I did so, and by fall the lost were accepting Christ and filling those churches. Because of that growth, the church offered to help fly me back on weekends if I would agree to stay. As I prayed, I felt led to stay on four years until they were ready for a full-time pastor. During the years in Missouri, those churches were among the fastest growing rural churches in the state. I was writing and sharing the dream with so many others who caught the vision and made it happen in their churches.

New Beginnings

"Weeping may last for a season, but joy comes in the morning." God is always in the miracle business. At a luncheon on a cold, rainy April day I was introduced to a retired Air Force sergeant, Jim Sims. He'd lost his wife to cancer several years before our meeting. Jim had a great compassion for people. We stayed in touch and eventually fell in love. Jim Sims and I were married and I moved to his home in Florida. The bishop said there were no churches open in Florida. I taught at a college and continued my research. Six miles north of our home, in the little community of Trilby, stood a one-room, unpainted church with only a tiny handful of people left. The church was located in one of Florida's highest crime areas and because of low attendance it was scheduled to close. Seven Methodist churches around it had already closed.

This time it was Jim who said, "Let's prove it with our lives!" I became the pastor of Trilby United Methodist Church. Six years later, those eight in attendance had grown to 350 members with debt-free buildings and a ministry that the Board of Global Ministries evaluated at a replacement cost of nearly a million dollars. Best of all, those buildings had been built and paid for without a fund raiser or a single negative vote. Jesus had been lifted up, and broken lives were mended. The Trilby Mission was packed with the African Americans, Anglos, and Hispanics who came for food, clothes, and our clinic. Our programs became wide-open doors and windows leading many of them to accept Christ. Teenagers and children who had accepted Christ shared their testimonies in a drama group week after week, leading many in attendance to Christ. A petition to the county brought a free health clinic and park. Singles, drama groups, country gospel nights, adult education, literacy programs, AA, a dinner-theater group, etc., opened windows of opportunity. I performed 20 weddings for couples from our singles group. After they found Christ, they found new beginnings.

The week the United Methodist Church gave me the Circuit Rider award, their highest award for church growth, I thought back to that holy ground in a Nebraska prairie country church yard. Wesley's foolproof method for church growth had never become outdated or ineffective. He had provided the ingredients that we never altered. What we did alter was the contemporary way in which we made them relevant to an America that was experiencing a moral and spiritual decline unparalleled in its history. Success is always a journey, not a destination. The road to success is always under construction.

Just as dying churches feel an urgency to survive, so the crisis in America has put our country in a survival mode. As big government declines and social programs are cut, what an opportunity for the church to fill the empty classrooms with purpose-driven programs! Family values and a return to old-fashioned morals and values are the talk of the town. To that end I will devote every fiber of my being and every moment for the rest of my life. Whatever happened to America during my lifetime, happened on my watch and yours. We are responsible. One person and God are a majority. We can make a difference.

As Bishop Earl Hunt dedicated our new buildings at Trilby, he said, "The problem of church growth is a simple problem. The only thing we have to do to get the church to grow is to help the church do more of what it is supposed to be doing all along. That is exactly what happened here. It happened because whenever the church of the Lord Jesus is turned loose in a community to help human beings and meet their needs and lift up the name of Jesus Christ, that church becomes indispensable in the community. There is a sign that should be hung over every church door. It should read, 'Broken lives mended here.' That is what happened here."

And it can happen anywhere! Wesley was right but you just have to prove it with your life. That is the price God exacts. Why offer God that which costs you nothing? After all, it isn't that life is so short, it is that eternity is so long. That is when nothing else will matter but the souls we have won and the lives we have touched. It will be worth it all! And now the worship is over and the service has begun. If you can dream it, you can do it!

Questions

1. In what ways does God expect the Church to grow?
2. What can we do to help the Church grow?

3. What do we do to prevent our churches from growing?
4. What part does prayer play in Church growth?
5. Is your church growing? Why or why not?
6. What might best help your church grow?
7. Describe your idea of the ideal church. What is the purpose of the ideal church?

Rose Sims   A Conference Evangelist for the United Methodist Church, Dr. Sims leads church growth, youth, singles, and women's seminars in this country and in places as diverse as Australia, Costa Rica, Ecuador, Cayman Islands, and England. In 1987 she won the United Methodist National Circuit Rider Award, Outstanding Pastor and Missionary. She received the Ed.D. from the University of Missouri and graduated from the St. Paul School of Theology. Her book New Life for Dying Churches: It Can Happen Anywhere! *won an international award and has been made into a video in cooperation with Ken Anderson Films and Dr. D. James Kennedy. Other books include* Papa Was a Promise Keeper *and books for children. She and Jim, her husband of 13 years, reside in Ridge Manor, Florida. She has five grown children.*

Conclusion

by Den Slattery and Gary Wales

A young man who had fought bravely for his country during World War I returned from the battlefield as a wounded, but decorated, soldier. His country had many economic and political problems that he felt could be solved with the right leadership. Filled with ambition, he eventually rose through the ranks to become one of the most powerful men of the twentieth century. His name was Adolf Hitler.

Today we wonder how Hitler was able to so captivate the nation of Germany that its citizens were willing to follow him into the unspeakable brutality of murdering over six million Jews and killing another 50 million people through his war efforts and programs of abortion, euthanasia, infanticide, and torture. Perhaps an even more important question is—Where was the Church? In a nation where virtually every baby was baptized, why didn't the Church oppose Hitler?

Strangely enough, the answer to that question has to do with TRUTH. For the path leading to Hitler's rise to power was paved many years before he was even born. Liberal and unbelieving German theologians threw out the great doctrines of the Christian faith long before Hitler rose to power. They denied the authority of Scripture, the deity of Jesus Christ, the miracles of the Bible, the sovereignty of God, the dignity of humans made in the image of God, and almost every other sacred truth of the early Church. God was demoted by the liberals of Germany, and man was deified. Man replaced God as the center of art, religion, history, literature, and philosophy. But when the liberal theologians exalted man, they opened the door to unrestrained evil. With God out of the way, there was no fear of judgment and, therefore, no need for the virtues of morality. Suddenly, there were no absolutes by which to govern life. The liberals exalted human reason and opinion, which they undergirded by raw power and brutal force. They believed in the survival of the fittest. In due time, the Church was also so weakened by its liberal leadership that the people had no idea what to believe anymore.

When Hitler finally arrived on the scene, the Church was so ignorant of the foundational truths of the faith that in many churches the Bible and the cross were removed from the altar and were replaced with Hitler's book, *Mein Kampf,* and a swastika. In the process, thousands of pastors swore allegiance to Hitler, who vowed to pay the Jews back for what they did to Jesus. The pastors justified their loyalty to Hitler as being their way of expressing patriotic duty to Germany.*

So what does that grim chapter in history have to do with us? Closely associated with the fall of Germany was the failure of the Church to preach and practice the truth. Currently, throughout the world, we are facing that same kind of dilemma because we don't understand the great truths of the Christian faith as recorded in the Bible. We talk about being inclusive and tolerating everything. We want to feel good about who we are without repenting and turning to Christ. We are told that our worship ser-

---

*Much of this information is taken from the book *Hitler's Cross* by Erwin Lutzer, Moody Press, Chicago: 1995.

vices need to be positive and upbeat, and that we should water down the truth so more people will attend. Therefore, many people in our churches don't have even the slightest grasp on what it means to be a Christian.

The *1992–1993 Barna Report* (Regal Books, 1992) found only 17% of Christians believed what the Bible says about attending church, sin, prayer, the Ten Commandments, the occult, and whether one needs to accept Christ to make it to heaven. Yet 80% of those Christians interviewed said they believed the Bible is the accurate, written Word of God. One conclusion we can make from that study is that there is a great ignorance about what the Bible teaches, since so many Christians seem to contradict it. Josh McDowell's book *Right From Wrong* (Word Publishing, 1994) is an analysis of a survey of 3,795 Christian young people between the ages of 11 and 18, all of whom have been raised in evangelical churches. Based on that study, 57% of those youth cannot affirm an objective standard of right and wrong. One of the big questions young people are asking today is, "What is truth?" Not knowing the answer to that question makes them 48% more likely to cheat on tests, 65% more likely to mistrust people, three times more likely to use illegal drugs, and six times more likely to attempt suicide (p. 18).

Therefore, it is vital for us to come to grips with the historic truths of the Christian faith so that we will not be deceived. Consider what Jesus said about truth:

"If you hold to my teaching, you are really my disciples. Then you will know the truth, and the truth will set you free" (John 8:31–32).

"I am the way and the truth and the life. No one comes to the Father except through me" (John 14:6).

Based on those statements, is it any wonder that truth is an important issue? If Jesus is the truth and knowing the truth is the only way we can be set free, then it stands to reason that embracing truth is of vital importance. Therefore, how can anyone claim to be a follower of Jesus who does not accept his teachings as truth but instead attempts to deceive others with lies that they substitute for the truth?

This book has been our feeble attempt to encourage the Church not to sacrifice the essential truths of the faith on the altar of cultural tolerance. It is our prayer that this book will be a reference guide that is kept close at hand and studied in churches around the world.

Where do you stand on these truths? They have been proclaimed for thousands of years in the Church as essential truths for all Christians. They are to be an anchor for our souls. We should memorize them and sing songs about them as did Martin Luther, John and Charles Wesley, John Newton, Fanny Crosby, and Isaac Watts. As Christians, we are the stewards in this generation of the truth of God, as was the Church of Hitler's day. Let's not make the same mistake that they made.

KNOW THE TRUTH

BELIEVE THE TRUTH

LIVE THE TRUTH

SHARE THE TRUTH